Meat Eats

Publisher & Creative Director: Nick Wells
Senior Editor: Cat Emslie
Designer: Lucy Robins
With thanks to: Lauren Perazza-Fontanez, Toria Lyle and Julie Pallot

This is a **FLAME TREE** Book

FLAME TREE PUBLISHING

Crabtree Hall, Crabtree Lane
Fulham, London SW6 6TY
United Kingdom
www.flametreepublishing.com

Flame Tree is part of The Foundry Creative Media Company Limited

First published 2008

09 11 12 10 08
3 5 7 9 10 8 6 4 2

ISBN: 978-1-84786-182-5

A copy of the CIP data for this book is available from the British Library.

Printed in China

Meat Eats

Quick and Easy, Proven Recipes

FLAME TREE
PUBLISHING

Contents

Hygiene in the Kitchen	10	Fried Rice with Chilli Beef	38
Nutrition	12	Szechuan Beef	40
Red Meat	16	Brandied Beef	42
Poultry & Game	20	Coconut Beef	44
		Chilli Beef	46
Beef	22	Beef & Baby Corn Stir Fry	48
		Beef Fajitas with Avocado Sauce	50
Spicy Beef Pancakes	24	Stir Fry Beef with Vermouth	52
Vietnamese Beef & Rice Noodle Soup	26	Beef with Paprika	54
Beef Noodle Soup	28	Beef Curry with Lemon & Arborio Rice	56
Colourful Beef in Lettuce	30	Chilli Beef Calzone	58
Shredded Chilli Beef	32	Cornish Pasties	60
Shredded Beef in Hoisin Sauce	34	Seared Calves' Liver with Onions & Mustard Mash	62
Sweet-&-Sour Shredded Beef	36	Chilli Con Carne with Crispy skinned Potatoes	64
		Grilled Steaks with Saffron Potatoes & Roast Tomatoes	66
		Ossobuco with Saffron Risotto	68
		Beef Teriyaki with Green & Black Rice	70
		Fettuccine with Calves' Liver & Calvados	72
		Pan-fried Beef with Creamy Mushrooms	74
		Meatballs with Olives	76
		Swedish Cocktail Meatballs	78
		Meatballs with Bean & Tomato Sauce	80
		Italian Meatballs in Tomato Sauce	82

Contents

Spaghetti & Meatballs — 84
Traditional Lasagne — 86
Spaghetti Bolognese — 88
Cannelloni with Spicy Bolognese Filling — 90
Fillet Steaks with Tomato & Garlic Sauce — 92
Veal Escallopes with Marsala Sauce — 94
Vitello Tonnato (Veal in Tuna Sauce) — 96
Italian Beef Pot Roast — 98
Italian Calf Liver — 100
Spicy Chilli Beef — 102
Pasta with Beef Capers & Olives — 104
Chinese Beef with Angel Hair Pasta — 106
Gnocchi with Tuscan Beef Ragu — 108

Lamb

Lamb — **110**

Kung-pao Lamb — 112
Lamb with Stir Fry Vegetables — 114
Lamb & Meatballs with Savoy Cabbage — 116
Spicy Lamb & Peppers — 118
Brandied Lamb Chops — 120
Lamb with Black Cherry Sauce — 122
Chilli Lamb — 124
Spicy Lamb in Yoghurt Sauce — 126
Lamb's Liver with Bacon & Onions — 128
Moroccan Lamb with Apricots — 130
Leg of Lamb with Minted Rice — 132
Lamb & Potato Moussaka — 134
Crown Roast of Lamb — 136
Lamb Pilaf — 138
Roast Leg of Lamb & Boulangère Potatoes — 140
Lancashire Hotpot — 142
Shepherd's Pie — 144
Red Wine Risotto with Lambs' Kidneys
    & Caramelised Shallots — 146
Marinated Lamb Chops with Garlic Fried Potatoes — 148
Pappardelle with Spicy Lamb & Peppers — 150
Lamb & Pasta Pie — 152
Roasted Lamb with Rosemary & Garlic — 154
Braised Lamb with Broad Beans — 156

Moroccan Penne	158
Lamb Arrabbiata	160
Creamed Lamb & Wild Mushroom Pasta	162
Tagliatelle with Creamy Liver & Basil	164

Pork

	166
Crispy Pork Wontons	168
Lion's Head Pork Balls	170
Barbecue Pork Steamed Buns	172
Sticky Braised Spareribs	174
Fried Pork-filled Wontons	176
Char Sui Pork & Noodle Salad	178

Dim Sum Pork Parcels	180
Pork with Tofu	182
Apple Tossed Pork	184
Pork Fried Noodles	186
Hoisin Pork	188
Pork Meatballs with Vegetables	190
Spicy Pork	192
Pork with Tofu & Coconut	194
Pork with Black Bean Sauce	196
Pork Spring Rolls	198
Special Fried Rice	200
Cashew & Pork Stir Fry	202
Barbecue Pork Fillets	204
Pork & Cabbage Parcels	206
Crispy Pork with Tangy Sauce	208
Caribbean Pork	210
Sausage & Bacon Risotto	212
Speedy Pork with Yellow Bean Sauce	214
Honey Pork with Rice Noodles & Cashews	216
Sweet-&-Sour Pork	218
Pork in Peanut Sauce	220
Pork with Spring Vegetables & Sweet Chilli Sauce	222
Pork with Assorted Peppers	224
Bacon, Mushroom & Cheese Puffs	226
Bacon & Tomato Breakfast Twist	228
Bacon & Split Pea Soup	230
Jamaican Jerk Pork with Rice & Peas	232

Contents

Pork Loin Stuffed with Orange & Hazelnut Rice 234
Pork Goulash & Rice 236
Nasi Goreng 238
Leek & Ham Risotto 240
Pork Sausages with Onion Gravy & Best-ever Mash 242
Roast Cured Pork Loin with Baked Sliced Potatoes 244
Spanish Style Pork Stew with Saffron Rice 246
New Orleans Jambalaya 248
Chinese Style Fried Rice 250
Tagliatelle with Stuffed Pork Escalopes 252
Oven Roasted Vegetables with Sausages 254
Hot Salami & Vegetable Gratin 256
Antipasto Penne 258

Italian Risotto 260
Oven-baked Pork Balls with Peppers 262
Pork Chop Hotpot 264
Cannelloni 266
Chorizo with Pasta in a Tomato Sauce 268
Pasta & Pork Ragu 270
Sausage & Redcurrant Pasta Bake 272
Pappardelle Pork with Brandy Sauce 274
Tagliatelle with Spicy Sausage Ragù 276
Gnocchi & Parma Ham Bake 278
Gammon with Red Wine Sauce & Pasta 280
Prosciutto & Gruyère Carbonara 282

Poultry & Game 284

Clear Chicken & Mushroom Soup 286
Creamy Caribbean Chicken & Coconut Soup 288
Chicken Noodle Soup 290
Chicken-filled Spring Rolls 292
Cantonese Chicken Wings 294
Deep-fried Chicken Wings 296
Orange-roasted Whole Chicken 298
Grilled Spiced Chicken with Tomato & Shallot Chutney 300
Lemon Chicken 302
Chicken in Black Bean Sauce 304
Chicken Chow Mein 306
Thai Coconut Chicken 308

Sauvigon Chicken & Mushroom Filo Pie	332
Chilli Roast Chicken	334
Cheesy Chicken Burgers	336
Chicken Cacciatore	338
Mexican Chicken	340
Chicken Marengo	342
Seared Duck with Pickled Plums	344
Crispy Aromatic Duck	346
Duck with Berry Sauce	348
Fried Ginger Rice with Soy Glazed Duck	350
Aromatic Duck Burgers on Potato Pancakes	352
Brown Rice & Lentil Salad with Duck	354
Duck Lasagne with Porcini & Basil	356
Lime & Sesame Turkey	358
Turkey Tetrazzini	360
Creamy Turkey & Tomato Pasta	362
Spaghetti with Turkey & Bacon Sauce	364
Baked Aubergines with Tomato & Mozzarella	366
Spatchcocked Poussins with Garlic Sage Butter	368
Guinea Fowl with Calvados & Apples	370
Pheasant with Portabella Mushrooms & Red Wine Gravy	372
Pheasant with Sage & Blueberries	374
Marinated Pheasant Breasts with Grilled Polenta	376
Rabbit Italian	378
Braised Rabbit with Red Peppers	380
Index	**382**

Stir–fried Chicken with Basil	310
Chicken & Cashew Nuts	312
Stir–fried Chicken with Spinach, Tomatoes & Pine Nuts	314
Chicken & Red Pepper Curried Rice	316
Chicken & Lamb Satay	318
Chicken Wraps	320
Sweet–&–Sour Rice with Chicken	322
Roast Chicken	324
Chicken with Roasted Fennel & Citrus Rice	326
Braised Chicken in Beer	328
Spicy Chicken Skewers with Mango Tabbouleh	330

Essential Hygiene in the Kitchen

It is well worth remembering that many foods can carry some form of bacteria. In most cases, the worst it will lead to is a bout of food poisoning or gastroenteritis, although for certain groups this can be more serious. The risk can be reduced or eliminated by good food hygiene and proper cooking.

Do not buy food that is past its sell-by date and do not consume any food that is past its use-by date. When buying food, use the eyes and nose. If the food looks tired, limp or a bad colour or it has a rank, acrid or simply bad smell, do not buy or eat it under any circumstances.

Regularly clean, defrost and clear out the refrigerator or freezer – it is worth checking the packaging to see exactly how long each product is safe to freeze.

Dish cloths and tea towels must be washed and changed regularly. Ideally use disposable cloths which should be replaced on a daily basis. More durable cloths should be

left to soak in bleach, then washed in the washing machine on a boil wash.

Always keep your hands, cooking utensils and food preparation surfaces clean and never allow pets to climb on to any work surfaces.

Buying

Avoid bulk buying where possible, especially fresh produce such as meat, poultry, fish, fruit and vegetables unless buying for the freezer. Fresh foods lose their nutritional value rapidly so buying a little at a time minimises loss of nutrients. It also eliminates a packed refrigerator which reduces the effectiveness of the refrigeration process.

When buying frozen foods, ensure that they are not heavily iced on the outside. Place in the freezer as soon as possible after purchase.

Preparation

Make sure that all work surfaces and utensils are clean and dry. Separate chopping boards should be used for raw and cooked meats, fish and vegetables. It is worth washing all fruits and vegetables regardless of whether they are going to be eaten raw or lightly cooked. Do not reheat food more than once.

All poultry must be thoroughly thawed before cooking. Leave the food in the refrigerator until it is completely thawed. Once defrosted, the chicken should be cooked as soon as possible. The only time food can be refrozen is when the food has been thoroughly thawed then cooked. Once the food has cooled then it can be frozen again for one month.

All poultry and game (except for duck) must be cooked thoroughly. When cooked the juices will run clear. Other meats, like minced meat and pork should be cooked right the way through. Fish should turn opaque, be firm in texture and break easily into large flakes.

Storing, Refrigerating and Freezing

Meat, poultry, fish, seafood and dairy products should all be refrigerated. The temperature of the refrigerator should be between 1–5°C/34–41°F while the freezer temperature should not rise above -18°C/-0.4°F. When refrigerating cooked food, allow it to cool down completely before refrigerating. Hot food will raise the temperature of the refrigerator and possibly affect or spoil other food stored in it.

Food within the refrigerator and freezer should always be covered. Raw and cooked food should be stored in separate parts of the refrigerator. Cooked food should be kept on the top shelves of the refrigerator, while raw meat, poultry and fish should be placed on bottom shelves to avoid drips and cross-contamination.

High-Risk Foods

Certain foods may carry risks to people who are considered vulnerable such as the elderly, the ill, pregnant women, babies and those suffering from a recurring illness. It is advisable to avoid those foods which belong to a higher-risk category.

There is a slight chance that some eggs carry the bacteria salmonella. Cook the eggs until both the yolk and the white are firm to eliminate this risk. Sauces including Hollandaise, mayonnaise, mousses, soufflés and meringues all use raw or lightly cooked eggs, as do custard-based dishes, ice creams and sorbets. These are all considered high-risk foods to the vulnerable groups mentioned above. Certain meats and poultry also carry the potential risk of salmonella and so should be cooked thoroughly until the juices run clear and there is no pinkness left. Unpasteurised products such as milk, cheese (especially soft cheese), pâté, meat (both raw and cooked) all have the potential risk of listeria and should be avoided.

When buying seafood, buy from a reputable source. Fish should have bright clear eyes, shiny skin and bright pink or red gills. The fish should feel stiff to the touch, with a slight smell of sea air and iodine. The flesh of fish steaks and fillets should be translucent with no signs of discolouration. Avoid any molluscs that are open or do not close when tapped lightly. Univalves such as cockles or winkles should withdraw into their shells when lightly prodded. Squid and octopus should have firm flesh and a pleasant sea smell.

Care is required when freezing seafood. It is imperative to check whether the fish has been frozen before. If it has been, then it should not be frozen again under any circumstances.

Nutrition
The Role of Essential Nutrients

A healthy and well-balanced diet is the body's primary energy source. In children, it constitutes the building blocks for future health as well as providing lots of energy. In adults, it encourages self-healing and regeneration within the body. A well-balanced diet will provide the body with all the essential nutrients it needs. This can be achieved by eating a variety of foods, demonstrated in the pyramid below:

Fats
milk, yoghurt
and cheese

Proteins
meat, fish, poultry, eggs,
nuts and pulses

*Fruits and
Vegetables*

Starchy Carbohydrates
cereals, potatoes, bread, rice and pasta

Fats

Fats fall into two categories: saturated and unsaturated fats. It is very important that a healthy balance is achieved within the diet. Fats are an essential part of the diet and a source of energy and provide essential fatty acids and fat soluble vitamins. The right balance of fats should boost the body's immunity to infection and keep muscles, nerves and arteries in good condition. Saturated fats are of animal origin and are hard when stored at room temperature. They can be found in dairy produce, meat, eggs, margarines and hard white cooking fat (lard) as well as in manufactured products such as pies, biscuits and cakes. A high intake of saturated fat over many years has been proven to increase heart disease and high blood cholesterol levels and often leads to weight gain. The aim of a healthy diet is to keep the fat content low in the foods that we eat. Lowering the amount of saturated fat that we consume is very important, but this does not mean that it is good to consume lots of other types of fat.

There are two kinds of unsaturated fats: poly-unsaturated fats and monounsaturated fats. Poly-unsaturated fats include the following oils: safflower oil, soybean oil, corn oil and sesame oil. Within the poly-unsaturated group are Omega oils. The Omega-3 oils are of significant interest because they have been found to be particularly beneficial to coronary health and can encourage brain growth and development. Omega-3 oils are derived from oily fish such as salmon, mackerel, herring, pilchards and sardines. It is recommended that we should eat these types of fish at least once a week. However, for those who do not eat fish or who are vegetarians, liver oil supplements are available in most supermarkets and health shops. It is suggested that these supplements should be taken on a daily basis. The most popular oils that are high in monounsaturates are olive oil, sunflower oil and peanut oil. The Mediterranean diet, which is based on a diet high in mono-unsaturated fats, is recommended for heart health. Also, monounsaturated fats are known to help reduce the levels of LDL (the bad) cholestrol.

Proteins

Composed of amino acids (proteins' building bricks), proteins perform a wide variety of essential functions for the body including supplying energy and building and repairing tissues. Good sources of proteins are eggs, milk, yoghurt, cheese, meat, fish, poultry, eggs, nuts and pulses. (See the second level of the pyramid.) Some of these foods, however, contain saturated fats. To strike a nutritional balance eat generous amounts of vegetable protein foods such as soya, beans, lentils, peas and nuts.

Fruits and Vegetables

Not only are fruits and vegetables the most visually appealing foods, but they are extremely good for us, providing essential vitamins and minerals essential for growth, repair and protection in the human body. Fruits and vegetables are low in calories and are responsible for regulating the body's metabolic processes and controlling the composition of its fluids and cells.

Minerals

CALCIUM Important for healthy bones and teeth, nerve transmission, muscle contraction, blood clotting and hormone function. Calcium promotes a healthy heart, improves skin, relieves aching muscles and bones, maintains the correct acid-alkaline balance and reduces menstrual cramps. Good sources are dairy products, small bones of small fish, nuts, pulses, fortified white flours, breads and green leafy vegetables.

CHROMIUM Part of the glucose tolerance factor, chromium balances blood sugar levels, helps to normalise hunger and reduce cravings, improves lifespan, helps protect DNA and is essential for heart function. Good sources are brewer's yeast, wholemeal bread, rye bread, oysters, potatoes, green peppers, butter and parsnips.

IODINE Important for the manufacture of thyroid hormones and for normal development. Good sources of iodine are seafood, seaweed, milk and dairy products.

IRON As a component of haemoglobin, iron carries oxygen around the body. It is vital for normal growth and development. Good sources are liver, corned beef, red meat, fortified breakfast cereals, pulses, green leafy vegetables, egg yolk and cocoa and cocoa products.

MAGNESIUM Important for efficient functioning of metabolic enzymes and development of the skeleton. Magnesium promotes healthy muscles by helping them to relax and is therefore good for PMS. It is also important for heart muscles and the nervous system. Good sources are nuts, green vegetables, meat, cereals, milk and yoghurt.

PHOSPHORUS Forms and maintains bones and teeth, builds muscle tissue, helps maintain the body's pH and aids metabolism and energy production. Phosphorus is present in almost all foods.

POTASSIUM Enables nutrients to move into cells, while waste products move out; promotes healthy nerves and muscles; maintains fluid balance in the body; helps secretion of insulin for blood sugar control to produce constant energy; relaxes muscles; maintains heart functioning and stimulates gut movement to encourage proper elimination. Good sources are fruit, vegetables, milk and bread.

SELENIUM Antioxidant properties help to protect against free radicals and carcinogens. Selenium reduces inflammation, stimulates the immune system to fight infections, promotes a healthy heart and helps vitamin E's action. It is also required for the male reproductive system and is needed for metabolism. Good sources are tuna, liver, kidney, meat, eggs, cereals, nuts and dairy products.

SODIUM Important in helping to control body fluid and balance, preventing dehydration. Sodium is involved in muscle and nerve function and helps move nutrients into cells. All foods are good sources, however processed, pickled and salted foods are richest in sodium.

ZINC Important for metabolism and the healing of wounds. It also aids ability to cope with stress, promotes a healthy nervous system and brain especially in the growing foetus, aids bones and teeth formation and is essential for constant energy. Good sources are liver, meat, pulses, whole-grain cereals, nuts and oysters.

Vitamins

VITAMIN A Important for cell growth and development and for the formation of visual pigments in the eye. Vitamin A comes in two forms: retinol and beta-carotenes. Retinol is found in liver, meat and meat products and whole milk and its products. Beta-carotene is a powerful antioxidant and is found in red and yellow fruits and vegetables such as carrots, mangoes and apricots.

VITAMIN B1 Important in releasing energy from carboydrate-containing foods. Good sources are yeast and yeast products, bread, fortified breakfast cereals and potatoes.

VITAMIN B2 Important for metabolism of proteins, fats and carbohydrates to produce energy. Good sources are meat, yeast extracts, fortified breakfast cereals and milk and its products.

VITAMIN B3 Required for the metabolism of food into energy production. Good sources are milk and milk products, fortified breakfast cereals, pulses, meat, poultry and eggs.

VITAMIN B5 Important for the metabolism of food and energy production. All foods are good sources but especially fortified breakfast cereals, whole-grain bread and dairy products.

VITAMIN B6 Important for metabolism of protein and fat. Vitamin B6 may also be involved with the regulation of sex hormones. Good sources are liver, fish, pork, soya beans and peanuts.

VITAMIN B12 Important for the production of red blood cells and DNA. It is vital for growth and the nervous system. Good sources are meat, fish, eggs, poultry and milk.

BIOTIN Important for metabolism of fatty acids. Good sources of biotin are liver, kidney, eggs and nuts. Micro-organisms also manufacture this vitamin in the gut.

VITAMIN C Important for healing wounds and the formation of collagen which keeps skin and bones strong. It is an important antioxidant. Good sources are fruits, soft summer fruits and vegetables.

VITAMIN D Important for absorption and handling of calcium to help build bone strength. Good sources are oily fish, eggs, whole milk and milk products, margarine and of course sufficient exposure to sunlight, as vitamin D is made in the skin.

VITAMIN E Important as an antioxidant vitamin helping to protect cell membranes from damage. Good sources are vegetable oils, margarines, seeds, nuts and green vegetables.

FOLIC ACID Critical during pregnancy for the development of the brain and nerves. It is always essential for brain and nerve function and is needed for utilising protein and red blood cell formation. Good sources are whole-grain cereals, fortified breakfast cereals, green leafy vegetables, oranges and liver.

VITAMIN K Important for controlling blood clotting. Good sources are cauliflower, Brussels sprouts, lettuce, cabbage, beans, broccoli, peas, asparagus, potatoes, corn oil, tomatoes and milk.

Carbohydrates

Carbohydrates are an energy source and come in two forms: starch and sugar carbohydrates. Starch carbohydrates are also known as complex carbohydrates and they include all cereals, potatoes, breads, rice and pasta. (See the fourth level of the pyramid). Eating whole-grain varieties of these foods also provides fibre. Diets high in fibre are believed to be beneficial in helping to prevent bowel cancer and can also keep cholesterol down. High-fibre diets are also good for those concerned about weight gain. Fibre is bulky so fills the stomach, therefore reducing hunger pangs. Sugar carbohydrates, which are also known as fast-release carbohydrates (because of the quick fix of energy they give to the body), include sugar and sugar-sweetened products such as jams and syrups. Milk provides lactose, which is a milk sugar, and fruits provide fructose, which is a fruit sugar.

Red Meat

Both home-grown and imported meat is readily available from supermarkets, butchers, farm shops and markets. Home-grown meat is normally more expensive than imported meat, often brought into the country frozen. Meat also varies in price depending on the cut. The more expensive and tender meats are usually those cuts that exercised less. They need a minimal amount of cooking and are suitable for roasting, grilling, griddling, frying and stir-frying. The cheaper cuts normally need longer, slower cooking and are used in casseroles and for stewing. Meat plays an important part in most people's diet, offering an excellent source of protein, B vitamins and iron.

When choosing meat, it is important to buy from a reputable source and to choose the correct cut for the cooking method. Look for meat that is lean without an excess of fat, is a good colour and has no unpleasant odour. If in doubt about the suitability of a cut, ask the butcher who should be happy to advise.

If buying frozen meat, allow to thaw before using. This is especially important for both pork and poultry. It is better to thaw meat slowly, lightly covered on the bottom shelf of the refrigerator. Use within 2–3 days of thawing, providing it has been kept in the refrigerator. If buying meat to freeze, do not freeze large joints in a home freezer as it will not be frozen quickly enough. Store thawed or fresh meat out of the supermarket wrappings, on a plate, lightly covered with greaseproof or baking paper and then wrap with cling film if liked. Do not secure the paper tightly round the meat as it needs to breathe. Ensure that the raw meat juices do not drip on to cooked foods. The refrigerator needs to be at a temperature of 5°C. Fresh meat such as joints, chops and steaks can be stored for up to three days. Mince, sausages and offal should be stored for only one day.

Different cultures and religion affect the way the meat has been killed and the carcass cut. The following is a description of different cuts of meat. They may be called by different names in different parts of the country.

Beef

When choosing beef, look for meat that is a good colour, with creamy yellow fat. There should be small flecks of fat (marbling) throughout, as this helps the meat to be tender. Avoid meat with excess gristle. Bright red beef means that the animal has been butchered recently, whereas meat that has a dark, almost purple, tinge is from meat that has been hung in a traditional manner. The darker the colour, the more tender and succulent.

RIB OR FORE RIB (1) Suitable for roasting. Sold either on or off the bone. Look for meat that is marbled for tenderness and succulence.

TOPSIDE (2) Suitable for pot roasting, roasting or braising. A lean, tender cut from the hindquarter.

SIRLOIN Suitable for roasting, grilling, frying, barbecuing or griddling. Sold boned or off the bone. A lean and tender cut from the back.

T-BONE STEAK Suitable for grilling, griddling, barbecuing or roasting. A tender, succulent cut taken from the fillet end of the sirloin.

TOP RIB Suitable for pot roasting or braising. Sold on or off the bone.

FILLET STEAK Suitable for grilling, frying, barbecuing or griddling. A whole fillet is used to make Châteaubriand, some say the best of all cuts. The most tender and succulent cut with virtually no fat. Comes from the centre of the sirloin.

RUMP (3) Suitable for grilling, frying, griddling or barbecuing. Not as tender as fillet of sirloin, but reputed to have more flavour.

SILVERSIDE (4) Suitable for boiling and pot roasts. Used to be sold ready-salted but is now normally sold unsalted.

FLASH-FRY STEAKS (5) Suitable for grilling, griddling or frying. Cut from the silverside, thick flank or topside.

BRAISING STEAK (6) Chuck, blade or thick rib, ideal for all braising or stews. Sold either in pieces or ready diced.

FLANK (7) Suitable for braising or stewing. A boneless cut from the mid- to hindquarter.

MINUTE STEAKS Suitable for grilling or griddling. Cut from the flank, a thin steak and beaten to flatten.

SKIRT Suitable for stewing or making into mince. A boneless, rather gristly cut.

BRISKET Suitable for slow roasting or pot roasting. Sold boned and rolled and can be found salted.

MINCE Suitable for meat sauces such as bolognese, also burgers, shepherd's pie and moussaka. Normally cut from clod, skirt, neck, thin rib or flank. Can be quite fatty. Steaks can also be minced if preferred to give a leaner mince. Sometimes referred to as ground beef.

OX KIDNEY Suitable for casseroles and stews. Strong flavour with hard central core that is discarded.

OXTAIL Suitable for casseroles or braising. Normally sold cut into small pieces.

Lamb

Lamb is probably at its best in the Spring, when the youngest lamb is available. It is tender to eat with a delicate flavour, and its flesh is a paler pink than the older lamb where the flesh is more red. The colour of the fat is also a good indication of age: young lamb fat is a very light, creamy colour. As the lamb matures, the fat becomes whiter and firmer. Imported lamb also has firmer, whiter fat. Lamb can be fatty so take care when choosing. It used to be possible to buy mutton (lamb that is at least one year old), but this now tends to be available only in specialist outlets. It has a far stronger, almost gamey flavour and the joints tend to be larger.

LEG (1) Suitable for roasting. Often sold as half legs and steaks cut from the fillet end. These can be grilled, griddled or barbecued. Steaks are very lean and need a little additional oil to prevent the meat from drying out.

SHANK Suitable for braising. A cut off the leg.

LOIN (2) Suitable for roasting. Sold on or off the bone, and can be stuffed and rolled. Can also be cut into chops, often as double loin chops which are suitable for grilling, griddling and barbecuing.

SHOULDER (3) Suitable for roasting. Can be sold boned, stuffed and rolled. Is fattier than the leg and has more flavour.

NOISETTE Suitable for grilling, griddling or barbecuing. A small boneless chop cut from the loin.

VALENTINE STEAK Suitable for grilling, griddling or barbecuing. Cut from a loin chop.

CHUMP CHOP (4) Suitable for grilling, griddling or barbecuing. Larger than loin chops and can be sold boneless.

BEST END OF NECK (5) Suitable for roasting, grilling or griddling. Sold as a joint or cutlets.

NECK FILLET Suitable for grilling or griddling. Sold whole or diced.

MIDDLE AND SCRAG END (6) Suitable for pot roasting, braising or stewing. A cheaper cut with a high ratio of fat and bone.

BREAST (7) Suitable for pot roast if boned, stuffed and rolled. Can be marinated and grilled or barbecued.

MINCE Suitable for burgers, pies, meat balls and for stuffing vegetables such as peppers. From various cuts and is often fatty.

LIVER Suitable for pan frying or grilling. Milder than ox or pig liver and cheaper than calves' liver.

KIDNEY Suitable for grilling, pan frying or casserole. Milder than ox or pig liver and normally sold encased in suet that is discarded.

Pork

Pork should be pale pink and slightly marbled. There should be a good layer of firm white fat with a thin elastic skin (rind) which can be scored before roasting to provide crackling. All cuts of pork are normally tender, as the pigs are slaughtered at an early age and nowadays are reared to be lean rather than fatty.

Pork used to be well-cooked, if not over-cooked, due to the danger of the parasite trichina. This no longer applies, however, and it is now recommended that the meat is cooked less to keep it moist and tender.

LEG (1) Suitable for roasting. Sold either on the bone or boned. Can be cut into chunks and braised or casseroled.

STEAKS (2) Suitable for grilling, frying, griddling or barbecue. A lean cut from the leg or the shoulder. Very tender but can be dry.

FILLET (or tenderloin) Suitable for roasting, pan frying, griddling or barbecuing. A tender cut, often sold already marinated.

LOIN (3) Suitable for roasting as a joint or cut into chops. Often sold with the kidney intact.

SHOULDER (4) Suitable for roasting. Often referred to as hand and spring, and sold cubed for casseroles and stews. A fatty cut.

SPARE RIBS Suitable for barbecuing, casseroles and roasting. Sold either as 'Chinese' where thin ribs are marinated then cooked, or 'American Style' ribs which are larger.

ESCALOPE Suitable for grilling, frying, griddling or barbecuing. Very lean and tender and requires very little cooking.

MINCE Suitable for burgers and meat balls. Is often from the cheaper cuts and can be fatty.

BELLY (5) Suitable for grilling or roasting. Is generally used to provide streaky bacon and is perhaps the fattiest cut of all.

LIVER Suitable for casseroles or frying. Stronger than lamb or calves' liver.

KIDNEY Suitable for casseroles or frying. Often sold as part of a loin chop. Stronger than lambs' kidneys.

Poultry & Game

Poultry relates to turkey, chicken, poussin, duck and geese. Most poultry is sold plucked, drawn and trussed. Due to extensive farming, chicken in particular offers a good source of cheap meat. However, there is a growing movement to return to the more traditional methods of farming. Organically-grown chickens offer a far more succulent bird with excellent flavour, although they tend to be a little more expensive. Both home-grown and imported poultry, fresh and frozen, are available. When buying fresh poultry, look for plump birds with a flexible breast bone, and no unpleasant odour or green tinge.

Frozen poultry should be rock hard with no ice crystals, as this could mean that the bird has thawed and been re-frozen. Avoid any produce where the packaging is damaged. When thawing, place in the refrigerator on a large plate and ensure that none of the juices drip on to other foods. Once thawed, remove all packaging, remove the giblets, if any, and reserve separately. Place on a plate and cover. Use within two days and ensure that the meat is thoroughly cooked and the juices run clear. Rest for 10 minutes before carving. When storing fresh poultry, place on a plate and cover lightly, allowing air to circulate. Treat as thawed poultry. Use within two days of cooking.

Poultry and game are low in saturated fat and provide a good source of protein as well as selenium. Remove the skin from poultry before eating if following a low-fat diet.

Poultry

TURKEY Whole birds are suitable for roasting. Traditionally served at Christmas, although with all the different cuts now available, turkey is eaten throughout the year.

CROWN The whole bird with the legs removed.

SADDLE Two turkey breast fillets, boned with the wings inserted.

BUTTERFLY The two breast fillets.

BREAST ROLL Boned breast meat, rolled and tied or contained in a net.

TURKEY PORTIONS are also available, ranging from breast steaks, diced thigh, escalopes, small whole breast fillets, drumsticks, wings and mince.

CHICKEN Suitable for all types of cooking: roasting, grilling, griddling, stewing, braising, frying and barbecuing. Also available in many different breeds and varieties, offering a good choice to the consumer. There are many cuts of chicken readily available: breast, wing and leg quarters which are still on the bone, drumsticks, thighs, breast fillets, escalopes (boneless, skinless portions), diced and stir-fry strips as well as mince.

CAPON Suitable for roasting. These are young castrated cockerels and are normally bred for their excellent flavour.

POUSSIN Suitable for roasting, grilling or casseroles. These are spring chickens and are 4–6 weeks old. They can be bought whole or spatchcocked – this is where the bird is split through the breast, opened up and secured on skewers. Normally serve two per person if small (450 g/1 lb) or one if larger (900 g/2 lb).

GUINEA FOWL Suitable for roasting or casseroles. Available all year round and about the same size as a pheasant, with a slightly gamey flavour. Most guinea fowl have already been hung and are sold ready for the table. When roasting, use plenty of fat or bacon as they can be dry.

GOOSE Suitable for roasting and often served as an alternative to turkey. Once dressed for the table, a goose will weigh around 4.5 kg/10 lb, but there is not much meat and this will serve around 6–8 people. It is very fatty, so pierce the skin well and roast on a trivet so the fat can be discarded or used for other cooking. Has a rich flavour, slightly gamey and a little like duck. Goose liver is highly prized and is used for foie gras.

DUCK Suitable for roasting, grilling, griddling and casseroles. Ducklings are normally used for the table and are between six weeks to three months old; ducks are not normally eaten. Duck has an excellent flavour but it is a fatty bird, so cook on a trivet as for goose. Available fresh or frozen and on average weighs 1.75–2.75 kg/4–6 lb. Also available in cuts, as boneless breast fillets, ideal for grilling or griddling, and leg portions, suitable for casseroles. The meat is also used to make pâté. There are quite a few varieties available, with perhaps the best well-known being the Aylesbury. Long Island, Peking and Barbary are also popular varieties.

Game

Game describes birds or animals which are hunted, not farmed, although some, such as pheasant, quails and rabbits, are now being reared domestically. Most game has a stronger flavour than poultry and is an acquired taste. When buying game, it is important to know its age, as this dictates the method of cooking. Normally sold oven-ready, it is advisable to buy from a reputable source who can guarantee the quality. Game which is less widely available includes partridge, grouse, quail, snipe and boar.

PIGEON Suitable for casseroles or stews, although young breast can be fried or grilled. Mainly only available from licensed sources.

PHEASANT Suitable for roasting or casseroles. Breast, which can be grilled, is also available. Pheasant needs to be well hung to give the best flavour.

RABBIT Suitable for casseroles, stews, pies, fricassée and roasting, or if young, frying. Sold whole or in portions, both with and without the bone, and available fresh and frozen. Soak in cold salted water for two hours before using, for a milder flavour .

HARE Suitable for casseroles. The most well-known recipe is Jugged Hare, where the blood is used to thicken the dish. Has a strong, gamey flavour. If a milder flavour is preferred, soak in cold water for up to 24 hours. Available from reputable game dealers.

VENISON Suitable for roasting, grilling, casseroles or making into sausages. The best joints for roasting are the saddle, haunch and shoulder, although the loin and fillet can also be used. All cuts benefit from marinating to help tenderise.

Beef

Spicy Beef Pancakes

SERVES 4

50 g/2 oz plain flour
pinch of salt
½ tsp Chinese five-
    spice powder
1 large egg yolk
150 ml/¼ pint milk
4 tsp sunflower oil
slices of spring onion,

to garnish

For the spicy beef filling:
1 tbsp sesame oil
4 spring onions, sliced
1 cm/½ inch piece fresh root
    ginger, peeled and grated
1 garlic clove, peeled

and crushed
300 g/11 oz sirloin steak,
    trimmed and cut into strips
1 red chilli, deseeded and
    finely chopped
1 tsp sherry vinegar
1 tsp soft dark brown sugar
1 tbsp dark soy sauce

Sift the flour, salt and Chinese five-spice powder into a bowl and make a well in the centre. Add the egg yolk and a little of the milk. Gradually beat in, drawing in the flour to make a smooth batter. Whisk in the rest of the milk.

Heat 1 teaspoon of the sunflower oil in a small heavy-based frying pan. Pour in just enough batter to thinly coat the base of the pan. Cook over a medium heat for 1 minute, or until the underside of the pancake is golden brown.

Turn or toss the pancake and cook for 1 minute, or until the other side of the pancake is golden brown. Make 7 more with the remaining batter. Stack them on a warmed plate as you make them, with greaseproof paper between each . Cover with foil and keep warm in a low oven.

Make the filling. Heat a wok or large frying pan, add the sesame oil and when hot, add the spring onions, ginger and garlic and stir-fry for 1 minute. Add the beef strips, stir-fry for 3–4 minutes, then stir in the chilli, vinegar, sugar and soy sauce. Cook for 1 minute, then remove from the heat.

Spoon one eighth of the filling over one half of each pancake. Fold the pancakes in half, then fold in half again. Garnish with a few slices of spring onion and serve immediately.

Try This: FOR AN ALTERNATIVE: 102   FOR A DIFFERENT MEAT OPTION: 124

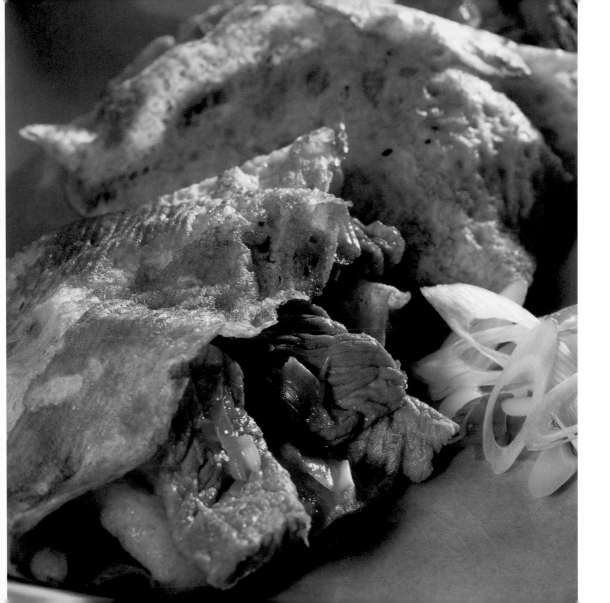

Vietnamese Beef & Rice Noodle Soup

SERVES 4–6

For the beef stock:
900 g/2 lb meaty beef bones
1 large onion, peeled and quartered
2 carrots, peeled and cut into chunks
2 celery stalks, trimmed and sliced
1 leek, washed and sliced into chunks

2 garlic cloves, unpeeled and lightly crushed
3 whole star anise
1 tsp black peppercorns

For the soup:
175 g/6 oz dried rice stick noodles
4–6 spring onions, trimmed and diagonally sliced

1 red chilli, deseeded and diagonally sliced
1 small bunch fresh coriander
1 small bunch fresh mint
350 g/12 oz fillet steak, very thinly sliced
salt and freshly ground black pepper

Place all the ingredients for the beef stock into a large stock pot or saucepan and cover with cold water. Bring to the boil and skim off any scum that rises to the surface. Reduce the heat and simmer gently, partially covered, for 2–3 hours, skimming occasionally. Strain into a large bowl and leave to cool, then skim off the fat. Chill in the refrigerator and when cold remove any fat from the surface. Pour 1.7 litres/3 pints of the stock into a large wok and reserve.

Cover the noodles with warm water and leave for 3 minutes, or until just softened. Drain, then cut into 10 cm/4 inch lengths.

Arrange the spring onions and chilli on a serving platter or large plate. Strip the leaves from the coriander and mint and arrange them in piles on the plate.

Bring the stock in the wok to the boil over a high heat. Add the noodles and simmer for about 2 minutes, or until tender. Add the beef strips and simmer for about 1 minute. Season to taste with salt and pepper. Ladle the soup with the noodles and beef strips into individual soup bowls and serve immediately with the plate of condiments handed around separately.

Try This: FOR AN ALTERNATIVE: 32   FOR A DIFFERENT MEAT OPTION: 290

Beef Noodle Soup

SERVES 4

900 g/2 lb boneless shin or
braising steak
1 cinnamon stick
2 star anise
2 tbsp light soy sauce
6 dried red chillies or 3

fresh, chopped in half
2 dried citrus peels, soaked
and diced (optional)
1.1 litre/2 pints beef or
chicken stock
350 g/12 oz egg noodles

2 spring onions, trimmed
and chopped, to garnish
warm chunks of crusty
farmhouse bread, to
serve (optional)

Trim the meat of any fat and sinew, then cut into thin strips. Place the meat, cinnamon, star anise, soy sauce, red chillies, chopped citrus peels (if using), and stock into the wok. Bring to the boil, then reduce the heat to a simmer. Skim any fat or scum that floats to the surface. Cover the wok and simmer for about 1½ hours or until the meat is tender.

Meanwhile, bring a saucepan of lightly salted water to the boil, then add the noodles and cook in the boiling water for 3–4 minutes until tender or according to packet directions. Drain well and reserve.

When the meat is tender, add the noodles to the wok and simmer for a further 1–2 minutes until the noodles are heated through thoroughly. Ladle the soup into warm shallow soup bowls or dishes and scatter with chopped spring onions. Serve, if liked, with chunks of warm crusty bread.

Try This: FOR AN ALTERNATIVE: 32   FOR A DIFFERENT MEAT OPTION: 26

Colourful Beef in Lettuce

SERVES 4

450 g/1 lb fresh beef mince
2 tbsp Chinese rice wine
1 tbsp light soy sauce
2 tsp sesame oil
2 tsp cornflour
25 g/1 oz Chinese
    dried mushrooms
2 tbsp groundnut oil
1 garlic clove, peeled
    and crushed

1 shallot, peeled and
    finely chopped
2 spring onions, trimmed
    and finely sliced
2 carrots, peeled and cut
    into matchsticks
125 g/4 oz canned bamboo
    shoots, drained and
    cut into matchsticks
2 courgettes, trimmed and

cut into matchsticks
1 red pepper, deseeded and
    cut into matchsticks
1 tbsp dark soy sauce
2 tbsp hoisin sauce
2 tbsp oyster sauce
4 large Iceberg lettuce leaves
sprigs of fresh flat-leaf
    parsley, to garnish

Place the beef mince in a bowl with 1 tablespoon of the Chinese rice wine, the light soy sauce, sesame oil and cornflour. Mix well and leave for 20 minutes.

Soak the dried mushrooms in almost boiling water for 20 minutes. Drain, rinse, drain again and squeeze out excess liquid. Trim and slice finely.

Heat a wok or large frying pan, add 1 tablespoon of the groundnut oil and when very hot, add the beef. Stir-fry for 1 minute, then remove using a slotted spoon. Reserve.

Wipe the wok clean and reheat. Add the remaining oil and when hot, add the garlic, shallot and spring onions and stir-fry for 10 seconds. Add the carrots and stir-fry for 1 minute. Add the mushrooms with the bamboo shoots, courgettes and pepper and stir-fry for 1 minute. Add the reserved beef, soy, hoisin and oyster sauces to the wok and stir-fry for 3 minutes.

Spoon the beef mixture on to lettuce leaves and fold into parcels. Garnish with flat-leaf parsley sprigs and serve.

Try This: FOR AN ALTERNATIVE: 68   FOR A DIFFERENT MEAT OPTION: 114

Shredded Chilli Beef

SERVES 4

450 g/1 lb lean beef steak, cut into very thin strips
1 tbsp Chinese rice wine
1 tbsp light soy sauce
2 tsp sesame oil
2 tsp cornflour
8 red chillies, deseeded
8 garlic cloves, peeled

225 g/8 oz onion, peeled and sliced
1 tsp Thai red curry paste
6 tbsp groundnut oil
2 red peppers, deseeded and sliced
2 celery stalks, trimmed and sliced

2 tbsp Thai fish sauce
1 tbsp dark soy sauce
shredded basil leaves and a sprig of fresh basil, to garnish
freshly cooked noodles, to serve

Place the beef in a bowl with the Chinese rice wine, light soy sauce, sesame oil and cornflour and mix well. Cover with clingfilm and leave to marinate in the refrigerator for 20 minutes, turning the beef over at least once.

Place the chillies, garlic, onion and red curry paste in a food processor and blend to form a smooth paste.

Drain the beef, shaking off any excess marinade. Heat a wok and add 3 tablespoons of the groundnut oil. When almost smoking, add the beef and stir-fry for 1 minute. Using a slotted spoon, remove the beef and reserve.

Wipe the wok clean, reheat and add the remaining oil. When hot add the chilli paste and stir-fry for 30 seconds. Add the peppers and celery with the fish sauce and dark soy sauce. Stir-fry for 2 minutes. Return the beef to the wok and stir-fry for a further 2 minutes or until the beef is cooked. Place into a warmed serving dish, sprinkle with shredded basil and a basil sprig and serve immediately with noodles.

Try This: FOR AN ALTERNATIVE: 34 FOR A DIFFERENT MEAT OPTION: 124

Shredded Beef in Hoisin Sauce

SERVES 4

2 celery sticks
125 g/4 oz carrots
450 g/1 lb rump steak
2 tbsp cornflour
salt and freshly ground
    black pepper

2 tbsp sunflower oil
4 spring onions, trimmed
    and chopped
2 tbsp light soy sauce
1 tbsp hoisin sauce
1 tbsp sweet chilli sauce

2 tbsp dry sherry
250 g pack fine egg
    thread noodles
1 tbsp freshly
    chopped coriander

Trim the celery and peel the carrots, then cut into fine matchsticks and reserve.

Place the steak between 2 sheets of greaseproof paper or baking parchment. Beat the steak with a meat mallet or rolling pin until very thin, then slice into strips. Season the cornflour with salt and pepper and use to coat the steak. Reserve.

Heat a wok, add the oil and when hot, add the spring onions and cook for 1 minute, then add the steak and stir-fry for a further 3–4 minutes, or until the meat is sealed.

Add the celery and carrot matchsticks to the wok and stir-fry for a further 2 minutes before adding the soy, hoisin and chilli sauces and the sherry. Bring to the boil and simmer for 2–3 minutes, or until the steak is tender and the vegetables are cooked.

Plunge the fine egg noodles into boiling water and leave for 4 minutes. Drain, then spoon on to a large serving dish. Top with the cooked shredded steak, then sprinkle with chopped coriander and serve immediately.

Try This: FOR AN ALTERNATIVE: 40 FOR A DIFFERENT MEAT OPTION: 168

Sweet–&–Sour Shredded Beef

SERVES 4

350 g/12 oz rump steak
1 tsp sesame oil
2 tbsp Chinese rice wine
    or sweet sherry
2 tbsp dark soy sauce
1 tsp cornflour
4 tbsp pineapple juice
2 tsp soft light brown sugar

1 tsp sherry vinegar
salt and freshly ground
    black pepper
2 tbsp groundnut oil
2 medium carrots, peeled
    and cut into matchsticks
125 g/4 oz mangetout,
    trimmed and cut

into matchsticks
1 bunch spring onions,
    trimmed and shredded
2 garlic cloves, peeled and
    crushed
1 tbsp toasted sesame seeds
freshly cooked Thai
    fragrant rice, to serve

Cut the steak across the grain into thin strips. Put in a bowl with the sesame oil, 1 tablespoon of the Chinese rice wine or sherry and 1 tablespoon of the soy sauce. Mix well, cover and leave to marinate in the refrigerator for 30 minutes.

In a small bowl, blend together the cornflour with the remaining Chinese rice wine or sherry, then stir in the pineapple juice, remaining soy sauce, sugar and vinegar. Season with a little salt and pepper and reserve.

Heat a wok until hot, add 1 tablespoon of the oil, then drain the beef, reserving the marinade, and stir-fry for 1–2 minutes, or until browned. Remove from the wok and reserve.

Add the remaining oil to the wok then add the carrots and stir-fry for 1 minute, then add the mangetout and spring onions and stir-fry for a further 1 minute.

Return the beef to the wok with the sauce, reserved marinade and garlic. Continue cooking for 1 minute or until the vegetables are tender and the sauce is bubbling. Turn the stir-fry into a warmed serving dish, sprinkle with toasted sesame seeds and serve immediately with the Thai fragrant rice.

Try This: FOR AN ALTERNATIVE: 52   FOR A DIFFERENT MEAT OPTION: 178

Fried Rice with Chilli Beef

SERVES 4

225 g/8 oz beef fillet	2 hot red chillies, deseeded	black pepper
375 g/12 oz long-grain rice	and finely chopped	2 tbsp milk
4 tbsp groundnut oil	2 tbsp light soy sauce	2 tbsp flour
3 onions, peeled and	2 tsp tomato paste	15 g/½ oz butter
thinly sliced	salt and freshly ground	2 medium eggs

Trim the beef fillet, discarding any fat, then cut into thin strips and reserve. Cook the rice in boiling salted water for 15 minutes or according to packet directions, then drain and reserve.

Heat a wok and add 3 tablespoons of oil. When hot, add 2 of the sliced onions and stir-fry for 2–3 minutes. Add the beef to the wok, together with the chillies, and stir-fry for a further 3 minutes, or until tender.

Add the rice to the wok with the soy sauce and tomato paste. Stir-fry for 1–2 minutes, or until piping hot. Season to taste with salt and pepper and keep warm. Meanwhile, toss the remaining onion in the milk, then the flour in batches. In a small frying pan fry the onion in the last 1 tablespoon of oil until crisp, then reserve.

Melt the butter in a small omelette pan. Beat the eggs with 2 teaspoons of water and pour into the pan. Cook gently, stirring frequently, until the egg has set, forming an omelette, then slide on to a clean chopping board and cut into thin strips. Add to the fried rice, sprinkle with the crispy onion and serve immediately.

Try This: FOR AN ALTERNATIVE: 46   FOR A DIFFERENT MEAT OPTION: 168

Szechuan Beef

SERVES 4

450 g/1 lb beef fillet
3 tbsp hoisin sauce
2 tbsp yellow bean sauce
2 tbsp dry sherry
1 tbsp brandy
2 tbsp groundnut oil
2 red chillies, deseeded and sliced
8 bunches spring onions, trimmed and chopped

2 garlic cloves, peeled and chopped
2.5 cm/1 inch piece fresh root ginger, peeled and cut into matchsticks
1 carrot, peeled, sliced lengthways and cut into short lengths
2 green peppers, deseeded and cut into 2.5 cm/

1 inch pieces
227 g can water chestnuts, drained and halved
sprigs of fresh coriander, to garnish
freshly cooked noodles with freshly ground Szechuan peppercorns, to serve

Trim the beef, discarding any sinew or fat, then cut into 5 mm/¼ inch strips. Place in a large shallow dish. In a bowl, stir the hoisin sauce, yellow bean sauce, sherry and brandy together until well blended. Pour over the beef and turn until coated evenly. Cover with clingfilm and leave to marinate for at least 30 minutes.

Heat a wok or large frying pan, add the oil and when hot, add the chillies, spring onions, garlic and ginger and stir-fry for 2 minutes or until softened. Using a slotted spoon, transfer to a plate and keep warm.

Add the carrot and peppers to the wok and stir-fry for 4 minutes or until slightly softened. Transfer to a plate and keep warm.

Drain the beef, reserving the marinade, add to the wok and stir-fry for 3–5 minutes or until browned. Return the chilli mixture, the carrot and pepper mixture and the marinade to the wok, add the water chestnuts and stir-fry for 2 minutes or until heated through. Garnish with sprigs of coriander and serve immediately with the noodles.

Try This: FOR AN ALTERNATIVE: 24 FOR A DIFFERENT MEAT OPTION: 112

Brandied Beef

SERVES 4

450 g/1 lb rump steak
2 tsp dark soy sauce
1 tsp soft dark brown sugar
salt and freshly ground
    black pepper
1 small fennel bulb

1 red pepper
1 orange
2 tbsp sunflower oil
15 g/½ oz unsalted butter
225 g/8 oz tiny whole button
    mushrooms

5 tbsp beef stock
3 tbsp brandy
orange wedges, to garnish
freshly cooked rice or
    noodles, to serve

Trim any fat from the steak and cut across the grain into thin strips. Place in a shallow bowl with the soy sauce, sugar and a little salt and pepper. Mix well and leave to marinate while preparing the vegetables.

Trim the fennel and slice as thinly as possible, from the stems down through the root. Quarter, deseed and thinly slice the red pepper. Thinly pare the rind from about half the orange and cut into fine matchsticks. Squeeze out the juice.

Heat the oil and butter in a wok, add the beef and stir-fry for 2 minutes, until brown and tender. Remove with a slotted spoon and reserve.

Add the fennel, red pepper and mushrooms to the wok and stir-fry for 3–4 minutes, or until softened. Add the orange zest and juice and the stock and cook for 2 minutes until the sauce is reduced slightly. Return the beef to the wok and stir-fry for 30 seconds to heat through.

Heat the brandy in a small saucepan or ladle, ignite, then let the flames subside and pour over the vegetables and meat. Gently shake the wok occasionally until the flames subside. Garnish with a few orange wedges and serve immediately with rice or noodles.

Try This: FOR AN ALTERNATIVE: 52   FOR A DIFFERENT MEAT OPTION: 120

Coconut Beef

SERVES 4

450 g/1 lb beef rump or
   sirloin steak
4 tbsp groundnut oil
2 bunches spring onions,
   trimmed and thickly sliced
1 red chilli, deseeded
   and chopped

1 garlic clove, peeled
   and chopped
2 cm/1 inch piece fresh root
   ginger, peeled and cut
   into matchsticks
125 g/4 oz shiitake
   mushrooms

200 ml/7 fl oz coconut cream
150 ml/¼ pint chicken stock
4 tbsp freshly chopped
   coriander
salt and freshly ground
   black pepper
freshly cooked rice, to serve

Trim off any fat or gristle from the beef and cut into thin strips. Heat a wok or large frying pan, add 2 tablespoons of the oil and heat until just smoking. Add the beef and cook for 5–8 minutes, turning occasionally, until browned on all sides. Using a slotted spoon, transfer the beef to a plate and keep warm.

Add the remaining oil to the wok and heat until almost smoking. Add the spring onions, chilli, garlic and ginger and cook for 1 minute, stirring occasionally. Add the mushrooms and stir-fry for 3 minutes. Using a slotted spoon, transfer the mushroom mixture to a plate and keep warm.

Return the beef to the wok, pour in the coconut cream and stock. Bring to the boil and simmer for 3–4 minutes, or until the juices are slightly reduced and the beef is just tender.

Return the mushroom mixture to the wok and heat through. Stir in the chopped coriander and season to taste with salt and pepper. Serve immediately with freshly cooked rice.

Try This: FOR AN ALTERNATIVE: 74   FOR A DIFFERENT MEAT OPTION: 194

Chilli Beef

SERVES 4

550 g/1¼ lb beef rump steak
2 tbsp groundnut oil
2 carrots, peeled and cut
    into matchsticks
125 g/4 oz mangetout,
    shredded

125 g/4 oz beansprouts
1 green chilli, deseeded
    and chopped
2 tbsp sesame seeds
freshly cooked rice, to serve

For the marinade:
1 garlic clove, peeled
    and chopped
3 tbsp soy sauce
1 tbsp sweet chilli sauce
4 tbsp groundnut oil

Using a sharp knife, trim the beef, discarding any fat or gristle, then cut into thin strips and place in a shallow dish. Combine all the marinade ingredients in a bowl and pour over the beef. Turn the beef in the marinade until coated evenly, cover with clingfilm and leave to marinate in the refrigerator for at least 30 minutes.

Heat a wok or large frying pan, add the groundnut oil and heat until almost smoking, then add the carrots and stir-fry for 3–4 minutes, or until softened. Add the mangetout and stir-fry for a further 1 minute. Using a slotted spoon, transfer the vegetables to a plate and keep warm.

Lift the beef strips from the marinade, shaking to remove any excess. Reserve the marinade. Add the beef to the wok and stir-fry for 3 minutes or until browned all over.

Return the stir-fried vegetables to the wok together with the beansprouts, chilli and sesame seeds and cook for 1 minute. Stir in the reserved marinade and stir-fry for 1–2 minutes or until heated through. Tip into a warmed serving dish or spoon on to individual plates and serve immediately with freshly cooked rice.

Try This: FOR AN ALTERNATIVE: 38   FOR A DIFFERENT MEAT OPTION: 222

Beef & Baby Corn Stir Fry

SERVES 4

3 tbsp light soy sauce
1 tbsp clear honey, warmed
450 g/1 lb beef rump steak,
    trimmed and thinly sliced
6 tbsp groundnut oil
125 g/4 oz shiitake
    mushrooms, wiped
    and halved
125 g/4 oz beansprouts, rinsed

2.5 cm/1 inch piece fresh
    root ginger, peeled and
    cut into matchsticks
125 g/4 oz mangetout,
    halved lengthways
125 g/4 oz broccoli, trimmed
    and cut into florets
1 medium carrot, peeled and
    cut into matchsticks

125 g/4 oz baby sweetcorn
    cobs, halved lengthways
¼ head Chinese leaves,
    shredded
1 tbsp chilli sauce
3 tbsp black bean sauce
1 tbsp dry sherry
freshly cooked noodles,
    to serve

Mix together the soy sauce and honey in a shallow dish. Add the sliced beef and turn to coat evenly. Cover with clingfilm and leave to marinate for at least 30 minutes, turning occasionally.

Heat a wok or large frying pan, add 2 tablespoons of the oil and heat until just smoking. Add the mushrooms and stir-fry for 1 minute. Add the bean sprouts and stir-fry for 1 minute. Using a slotted spoon, transfer the mushroom mixture to a plate and keep warm.

Drain the beef, reserving the marinade. Reheat the wok, pour in 2 tablespoons of the oil and heat until smoking. Add the beef and stir-fry for 4 minutes or until browned. Transfer to a plate and keep warm.

Add the remaining oil to the wok and heat until just smoking. Add the ginger, mangetout, broccoli, carrot and the baby sweetcorn with the shredded Chinese leaves and stir-fry for 3 minutes. Stir in the chilli and black bean sauces, the sherry, the reserved marinade and the beef and mushroom mixture. Stir-fry for 2 minutes, then serve immediately with freshly cooked noodles.

Try This: FOR AN ALTERNATIVE: 106   FOR A DIFFERENT MEAT OPTION: 114

Beef Fajitas with Avocado Sauce

SERVES 3–6

2 tbsp sunflower oil
450 g/1 lb beef fillet or rump
   steak, trimmed and cut
   into thin strips
2 garlic cloves, peeled
   and crushed
1 tsp ground cumin
¼ tsp cayenne pepper

1 tbsp paprika
230 g can chopped tomatoes
215 g can red kidney beans,
   drained
1 tbsp freshly chopped
   coriander
1 avocado, peeled, pitted
   and chopped

1 shallot, peeled and chopped
1 large tomato, skinned,
   deseeded and chopped
1 red chilli, diced
1 tbsp lemon juice
6 large flour tortilla pancakes
3–4 tbsp soured cream
green salad, to serve

Heat the wok, add the oil, then stir-fry the beef for 3–4 minutes. Add the garlic and spices and continue to cook for a further 2 minutes. Stir the tomatoes into the wok, bring to the boil, cover and simmer gently for 5 minutes.

Meanwhile, blend the kidney beans in a food processor until slightly broken up, then add to the wok. Continue to cook for a further 5 minutes, adding 2–3 tablespoons of water. The mixture should be thick and fairly dry. Stir in the chopped coriander.

Mix the chopped avocado, shallot, tomato, chilli and lemon juice together. Spoon into a serving dish and reserve.

When ready to serve, warm the tortillas and spread with a little soured cream. Place a spoonful of the beef mixture on top, followed by a spoonful of the avocado sauce, then roll up. Repeat until all the mixture is used up. Serve immediately with a green salad.

Try This: FOR AN ALTERNATIVE: 58   FOR A DIFFERENT MEAT OPTION: 126

Stir–fried Beef with Vermouth

SERVES 4

350 g/12 oz beef steak, such
  as rump or sirloin
2 tbsp plain flour
salt and freshly ground
  black pepper
3 tbsp sunflower oil

2 shallots, peeled and
  finely chopped
125 g/4 oz button
  mushrooms, wiped
  and halved
2 tbsp freshly

chopped tarragon
3 tbsp dry vermouth or
  Martini
150 ml/¼ pint single cream
125 g/4 oz stir-fry noodles
2 tsp sesame oil

Trim the beef and cut into thin strips. Place the flour in a bowl and add salt and pepper to taste, then stir well. Add the beef and stir until well coated, then remove from the flour and reserve.

Heat a wok, then add the oil and when hot, add the shallots and stir-fry for 2 minutes. Add the beef strips and stir-fry for 3–4 minutes before adding the mushrooms and 1 tablespoon of the chopped tarragon. Stir-fry for a further 1 minute.

Pour in the vermouth or Martini, stirring continuously, then add the cream. Cook for 2–3 minutes, or until the sauce is slightly thickened and the meat is cooked thoroughly. Adjust the seasoning and keep warm.

Meanwhile, place the noodles in a saucepan and cover with boiling water. Leave to stand for 4 minutes, then drain thoroughly and return to the wok. Add the sesame oil to the noodles and stir-fry for 1–2 minutes, or until heated through thoroughly. Pile the noodles on to serving dishes, top with the beef and serve immediately.

Try This: FOR AN ALTERNATIVE: 36   FOR A DIFFERENT MEAT OPTION: 114

Beef with Paprika

SERVES 4

700 g/1½ lb rump steak
3 tbsp plain flour
salt and freshly ground
    black pepper
1 tbsp paprika
350 g/12 oz long-grain rice

75 g/3 oz butter
1 tsp vegetable oil
1 onion, peeled and thinly
    sliced into rings
225 g/8 oz button mushrooms,
    wiped and sliced

2 tsp dry sherry
150 ml/¼ pint soured cream
2 tbsp freshly snipped chives
bundle of chives, to garnish

Beat the steak until very thin, then trim off and discard the fat and cut into thin strips. Season the flour with the salt, pepper and paprika, then toss the steak in the flour until coated.

Meanwhile, place the rice in a saucepan of boiling salted water and simmer for 15 minutes until tender or according to packet directions. Drain the rice, then return to the saucepan, add 25 g/1 oz of the butter, cover and keep warm.

Heat the wok, then add the oil and 25 g/1 oz of the butter. When hot, stir-fry the meat for 3–5 minutes until sealed. Remove from the wok with a slotted spoon and reserve. Add the remaining butter to the wok and stir-fry the onion rings and button mushrooms for 3–4 minutes.

Add the sherry while the wok is very hot, then turn down the heat. Return the steak to the wok with the soured cream and seasoning to taste. Heat through until piping hot, then sprinkle with the snipped chives. Garnish with bundles of chives and serve immediately with the cooked rice.

Try This: FOR AN ALTERNATIVE: 64   FOR A DIFFERENT MEAT OPTION: 118

Beef Curry with Lemon & Arborio Rice

SERVES 4

450 g/1 lb beef fillet
1 tbsp olive oil
2 tbsp green curry paste
1 green pepper, deseeded
    and cut into strips
1 red pepper, deseeded
    and cut into strips
1 celery stick, trimmed
    and sliced
juice of 1 fresh lemon
2 tsp Thai fish sauce
2 tsp demerara sugar
225 g/8 oz Arborio rice
15 g/½ oz butter
2 tbsp freshly
    chopped coriander
4 tbsp crème fraîche

Trim the beef fillet, discarding any fat, then cut across the grain into thin slices. Heat a wok, add the oil and when hot, add the green curry paste and cook for 30 seconds. Add the beef strips and stir-fry for 3–4 minutes.

Add the sliced peppers and the celery and continue to stir-fry for 2 minutes. Add the lemon juice, Thai fish sauce and sugar and cook for a further 3–4 minutes, or until the beef is tender and cooked to personal preference.

Meanwhile, cook the Arborio rice in a saucepan of lightly salted boiling water for 15–20 minutes, or until tender. Drain, rinse with boiling water and drain again. Return to the saucepan and add the butter. Cover and allow the butter to melt before turning it out on to a large serving dish. Sprinkle the cooked curry with the chopped coriander and serve immediately with the rice and crème fraîche.

Try This: FOR AN ALTERNATIVE: 102   FOR A DIFFERENT MEAT OPTION: 122

Chilli Beef Calzone

SERVES 4

Basic pizza dough:
225 g/8 oz strong plain flour
½ tsp salt
¼ tsp quick-acting dried
    yeast
150 ml/¼ pint warm water

1 tbsp extra-virgin olive oil

For the filling:
1 tbsp sunflower oil
1 onion, peeled and
    finely chopped

1 green pepper, deseeded
    and chopped
225 g/8 oz minced beef steak
420 g can chilli beans
220 g can chopped tomatoes
mixed salad leaves, to serve

Preheat the oven to 220°C/425°F/Gas Mark 7, 15 minutes before baking. To make the dough, sift the flour and salt into a bowl and stir in the yeast. Make a well in the centre and gradually add the water and oil to form soft dough. Knead the dough on a floured surface for about 5 minutes until smooth and elastic. Place in a lightly oiled bowl and cover with clingfilm. Leave to rise in a warm place for 1 hour.

Heat the oil in a large saucepan and gently cook the onion and pepper for 5 minutes. Add the minced beef to the saucepan and cook for 10 minutes, until browned.

Add the chilli beans and tomatoes and simmer gently for 30 minutes, or until the mince is tender. Place a baking sheet into the preheated oven to heat up.

Divide the pizza dough into 4 equal pieces. Cover 3 pieces of the dough with clingfilm and roll out the other piece on a lightly floured board to a 20.5 cm/8 inch round.

Spoon a quarter of the chilli mixture on to half of the dough round and dampen the edges with a little water. Fold over the empty half of the dough and press the edges together well to seal. Repeat this process with the remaining dough. Place on the hot baking sheet and bake for 15 minutes. Serve with the salad leaves.

Try This: FOR AN ALTERNATIVE: 24   FOR A DIFFERENT MEAT OPTION: 192

Cornish Pasties

SERVES 4

For the pastry:
350 g/12 oz self-raising flour
75 g/3 oz butter or margarine
75 g/3 oz lard or white
    vegetable fat
salt and freshly ground
    black pepper

For the filling:
550 g/1¼ lb braising steak,
    very finely chopped
1 large onion, peeled and
    finely chopped
1 large potato, peeled
    and diced
200 g/7 oz swede, peeled

and diced
3 tbsp Worcestershire sauce
1 small egg, beaten, to glaze

To garnish:
tomato slices or wedges
sprigs of fresh parsley

Preheat the oven to 180°C/350°F/Gas Mark 4, about 15 minutes before required. To make the pastry, sift the flour into a large bowl and add the fats, chopped into little pieces. Rub the fats and flour together until the mixture resembles coarse breadcrumbs. Season to taste with salt and pepper and mix again.

Add about 2 tablespoons of cold water, a little at a time, and mix until the mixture comes together to form a firm but pliable dough. Turn on to a lightly floured surface, knead until smooth, then wrap and chill in the refrigerator.

To make the filling, put the braising steak in a large bowl with the onion. Add the potatoes and swede to the bowl together with the Worcestershire sauce and salt and pepper. Mix well.

Divide the dough into 8 balls and roll each ball into a circle about 25.5 cm/10 inches across. Divide the filling between the circles of pastry. Wet the edge of the pastry, then fold over the filling. Pinch the edges to seal. Transfer the pasties to a lightly oiled baking sheet. Make a couple of small holes in each pasty and brush with beaten egg. Cook in the preheated oven for 15 minutes, remove and brush again with the egg. Return to the oven for a further 15–20 minutes until golden. Cool slightly, garnish with tomato and parsley and serve.

Try This: FOR AN ALTERNATIVE: 58   FOR A DIFFERENT MEAT OPTION: 226

Seared Calves' Liver with Onions & Mustard Mash

SERVES 2

2 tbsp olive oil
100 g/3½ oz butter
3 large onions, peeled
    and finely sliced
pinch of sugar
salt and freshly ground

black pepper
1 tbsp sprigs of fresh thyme
1 tbsp balsamic vinegar
700 g/1½ lb potatoes, peeled
    and cut into chunks
6–8 tbsp milk

1 tbsp wholegrain mustard
3–4 fresh sage leaves
550 g/1¼ lb thinly sliced
    calves' liver
1 tsp lemon juice

Preheat the oven to 150°C/300°F/Gas Mark 2. Heat half the oil and 25 g/1 oz of the butter in a flameproof casserole. When foaming, add the onions. Cover and cook over a low heat for 20 minutes until softened and beginning to collapse. Add the sugar and season with salt and pepper. Stir in the thyme. Cover the casserole and transfer to the preheated oven. Cook for a further 30–45 minutes until softened completely, but not browned. Remove from the oven and stir in the balsamic vinegar.

Meanwhile, boil the potatoes in boiling salted water for 15–18 minutes until tender. Drain well, then return to the pan. Place over a low heat to dry completely, remove from the heat and stir in 50 g/2 oz of the butter, the milk, mustard and salt and pepper to taste. Mash thoroughly until creamy and keep warm.

Heat a large frying pan and add the remaining butter and oil. When it is foaming, add the mustard and sage leaves and stir for a few seconds, then add the liver. Cook over a high heat for 1–2 minutes on each side. It should remain slightly pink: do not overcook. Remove the liver from the pan. Add the lemon juice to the pan and swirl around to deglaze.

To serve, place a large spoonful of the mashed potato on each plate. Top with some of the melting onions, the liver and finally the pan juices.

Try This: FOR AN ALTERNATIVE: 72 FOR A DIFFERENT MEAT OPTION: 128

Chilli Con Carne with Crispy–skinned Potatoes

SERVES 4

2 tbsp vegetable oil, plus extra for brushing
1 large onion, peeled and finely chopped
1 garlic clove, peeled and finely chopped
1 red chilli, deseeded and finely chopped

450 g/1 lb chuck steak, finely chopped, or lean beef mince
1 tbsp chilli powder
400 g can chopped tomatoes
2 tbsp tomato purée
400 g can red kidney beans, drained and rinsed

4 large baking potatoes
coarse salt and freshly ground black pepper

To serve:
ready-made guacamole
soured cream

Preheat the oven to 150°C/300°F/Gas Mark 2. Heat the oil in a large flameproof casserole and add the onion. Cook gently for 10 minutes until soft and lightly browned. Add the garlic and chilli and cook briefly. Increase the heat. Add the chuck steak or lean mince and cook for a further 10 minutes, stirring occasionally, until browned.

Add the chilli powder and stir well. Cook for about 2 minutes, then add the chopped tomatoes and tomato purée. Bring slowly to the boil. Cover and cook in the preheated oven for 1½ hours. Meanwhile, brush a little vegetable oil all over the potatoes and rub on some coarse salt. Put the potatoes in the oven alongside the chilli.

When the 1½ hours are up, remove the chilli from the oven and stir in the kidney beans. Return to the oven for a further 15 minutes.

Remove the chilli and potatoes from the oven. Cut a cross in each potato, then squeeze to open slightly and season to taste with salt and pepper. Serve with the chilli, guacamole and soured cream.

Try This: FOR AN ALTERNATIVE: 46   FOR A DIFFERENT MEAT OPTION: 124

Grilled Steaks with Saffron Potatoes & Roast Tomatoes

SERVES 4

700 g/1½ lb new potatoes, halved
few strands of saffron
300 ml/½ pint vegetable or beef stock
1 small onion, peeled and finely chopped
75 g/3 oz butter
salt and freshly ground black pepper
2 tsp balsamic vinegar
2 tbsp olive oil
1 tsp caster sugar
8 plum tomatoes, halved
4 boneless sirloin steaks, each weighing 225 g/8 oz
2 tbsp freshly chopped parsley

Cook the potatoes in boiling salted water for 8 minutes and drain well. Return the potatoes to the saucepan along with the saffron, stock, onion and 25 g/1 oz of the butter. Season to taste with salt and pepper and simmer uncovered for 10 minutes until the potatoes are tender.

Meanwhile, preheat the grill to medium. Mix together the vinegar, olive oil, sugar and seasoning. Arrange the tomatoes cut-side up in a foil-lined grill pan and drizzle over the dressing. Grill for 12–15 minutes, basting occasionally, until tender.

Melt the remaining butter in a frying pan. Add the steaks and cook for 4–8 minutes to taste and depending on thickness.

Arrange the potatoes and tomatoes in the centre of 4 serving plates. Top with the steaks along with any pan juices. Sprinkle over the parsley and serve immediately.

Try This: FOR AN ALTERNATIVE: 62   FOR A DIFFERENT MEAT OPTION: 242

Ossobuco with Saffron Risotto

SERVES 4

125 g/4 oz butter
2 tbsp olive oil
4 large pieces of shin of veal
   (often sold as ossobuco)
2 onions, peeled and
   roughly chopped
2 garlic cloves, peeled and
   finely chopped

300 ml/½ pint white wine
5 plum tomatoes, peeled
   and chopped
1 tbsp tomato purée
salt and freshly ground
   black pepper
2 tbsp freshly
   chopped parsley

grated rind of 1 small lemon
few strands of saffron, crushed
350 g/12 oz Arborio rice
1.3 litres/2¼ pints chicken
   stock, heated
50 g/2 oz Parmesan
   cheese, grated

Heat 50 g/2 oz butter with half the oil in a large saucepan and add the pieces of veal. Brown lightly on both sides, then transfer to a plate. Add half the onion and garlic and cook gently for about 10 minutes until the onion is just golden.

Return the veal to the saucepan along with the white wine, tomatoes and tomato purée. Season lightly with salt and pepper, cover and bring to a gentle simmer. Cook very gently for 1 hour. Uncover and cook for a further 30 minutes until the meat is cooked and the sauce is reduced and thickened. Season to taste. Mix together the remaining garlic, parsley and lemon rind and reserve.

Meanwhile, slowly melt the remaining butter and oil in a large deep-sided frying pan. Add the remaining onion and cook gently for 5–7 minutes until just brown. Add the saffron and stir for a few seconds, then add the rice. Cook for a further minute until the rice is well coated in oil and butter.

Begin adding the stock a ladleful at a time, stirring well after each addition of stock and waiting until it is absorbed before adding the next. Continue in this way until all the stock is used. Remove from the heat and stir in the grated Parmesan cheese and seasoning. Spoon a little of the saffron risotto on to each of 4 serving plates. Top with the ossobuco and sauce and sprinkle over the reserved garlic and parsley mixture. Serve immediately.

Try This: FOR AN ALTERNATIVE: 94   FOR A DIFFERENT MEAT OPTION: 260

Beef Teriyaki with Green & Black Rice

SERVES 4

3 tbsp sake (Japanese
   rice wine)
3 tbsp dry sherry
3 tbsp dark soy sauce
1½ tbsp soft brown sugar

4 sirloin steaks, each weighing
   175 g/6 oz, trimmed
350 g/12 oz long-grain and
   wild rice
2.5 cm/1 inch piece fresh

   root ginger
225 g/8 oz mangetout
salt
6 spring onions, trimmed
   and cut into fine strips

In a small saucepan, gently heat the sake, dry sherry, dark soy sauce and sugar until the sugar has dissolved. Increase the heat and bring to the boil. Remove from the heat and leave until cold. Lightly wipe the steaks, place in a shallow dish and pour the sake mixture over. Cover loosely and leave to marinate in the refrigerator for at least 1 hour, spooning the marinade over the steaks occasionally.

Cook the rice with the piece of root ginger, according to the packet instructions. Drain well, then remove and discard the piece of ginger.

Slice the mangetout thinly lengthways into fine shreds. Plunge into a saucepan of boiling salted water, return the water to the boil and drain immediately. Stir the drained mangetout and spring onions into the hot rice.

Meanwhile, heat a griddle pan until almost smoking. Remove the steaks from the marinade and cook on the hot pan for 3–4 minutes each side, depending on the thickness.

Place the remaining marinade in a saucepan and bring to the boil. Simmer rapidly for 2 minutes and remove from the heat. When the steaks are cooked to personal preference, leave to rest for 2–3 minutes, then slice thinly and serve with the rice and the hot marinade.

Try This: FOR AN ALTERNATIVE: 68   FOR A DIFFERENT MEAT OPTION: 212

Fettuccine with Calves' Liver & Calvados

SERVES 4

450 g/1 lb calves' liver,
    trimmed and thinly sliced
50 g/2 oz plain flour
salt and freshly ground
    black pepper

1 tsp paprika
50 g/2 oz butter
1½ tbsp olive oil
2 tbsp Calvados
150 ml/¼ pint cider

150 ml/¼ pint
    whipping cream
350 g/12 oz fresh fettuccine
fresh thyme sprigs,
    to garnish

Season the flour with the salt, black pepper and paprika, then toss the liver in the flour until well coated.

Melt half the butter and 1 tablespoon of the olive oil in a large frying pan and fry the liver in batches for 1 minute, or until just browned but still slightly pink inside. Remove using a slotted spoon and place in a warmed dish.

Add the remaining butter to the pan, stir in 1 tablespoon of the seasoned flour and cook for 1 minute. Pour in the Calvados and cider and cook over a high heat for 30 seconds. Stir the cream into the sauce and simmer for 1 minute to thicken slightly, then season to taste. Return the liver to the pan and heat through.

Bring a large pan of lightly salted water to a rolling boil. Add the fettuccine and cook according to the packet instructions, about 3–4 minutes, or until 'al dente'.

Drain the fettuccine thoroughly, return to the pan and toss in the remaining olive oil. Divide among 4 warmed plates and spoon the liver and sauce over the pasta. Garnish with thyme sprigs and serve immediately.

Try This: FOR AN ALTERNATIVE: 62   FOR A DIFFERENT MEAT OPTION: 274

Pan–fried Beef with Creamy Mushrooms

SERVES 4

225 g/8 oz shallots, peeled
2 garlic cloves, peeled
2 tbsp olive oil
4 medallions of beef
4 plum tomatoes

125 g/4 oz flat mushrooms
3 tbsp brandy
150 ml/¼ pint red wine
salt and freshly ground
    black pepper

4 tbsp double cream

To serve:
baby new potatoes
freshly cooked green beans

Cut the shallots in half if large, then chop the garlic. Heat the oil in a large frying pan and cook the shallots for about 8 minutes, stirring occasionally, until almost softened. Add the garlic and beef and cook for 8–10 minutes, turning once during cooking until the meat is browned all over. Using a slotted spoon, transfer the beef to a plate and keep warm.

Rinse the tomatoes and cut into eighths, then wipe the mushrooms and slice. Add to the pan and cook for 5 minutes, stirring frequently until the mushrooms have softened.

Pour in the brandy and heat through. Draw the pan off the heat and carefully ignite. Allow the flames to subside. Pour in the wine, return to the heat and bring to the boil. Boil until reduced by one third. Draw the pan off the heat, season to taste with salt and pepper, add the cream and stir.

Arrange the beef on serving plates and spoon over the sauce. Serve with baby new potatoes and a few green beans.

Try This: FOR AN ALTERNATIVE: 66   FOR A DIFFERENT MEAT OPTION: 162

Meatballs with Olives

SERVES 4

250 g/9 oz shallots, peeled
2–3 garlic cloves, peeled and
 crushed
450 g/1 lb minced beef steak
2 tbsp fresh white or
 wholemeal breadcrumbs
3 tbsp freshly chopped basil
salt and freshly ground

black pepper
2 tbsp olive oil
5 tbsp ready-made
 pesto sauce
5 tbsp mascarpone cheese
50 g/2 oz pitted black
 olives, halved
275 g/10 oz thick pasta

noodles, e.g. tagliatelle
freshly chopped flat-leaf
 parsley
sprigs of fresh flat-leaf
 parsley, to garnish
freshly grated Parmesan
 cheese, to serve

Chop 2 of the shallots finely and place in a bowl with the garlic, beef, breadcrumbs, basil and seasoning to taste. With damp hands, bring the mixture together and shape into small balls about the size of an apricot.

Heat the olive oil in a frying pan and cook the meatballs for 8–10 minutes, turning occasionally, until browned and the beef is tender. Remove and drain on absorbent kitchen paper.

Slice the remaining shallots, add to the pan and cook for 5 minutes, until softened. Blend the pesto and mascarpone together, then stir into the pan with the olives. Bring to the boil, reduce the heat and return the meatballs to the pan. Simmer for 5–8 minutes, or until the sauce has thickened and the meatballs are cooked thoroughly.

Meanwhile, bring a large saucepan of lightly salted water to the boil and cook the noodles for 8–10 minutes, or 'al dente'. Drain the noodles, reserving 2 tablespoons of the cooking liquor. Return the noodles to the pan with the reserved cooking liquor and pour in the sauce. Stir the noodles, then sprinkle with chopped parsley. Garnish with a few sprigs of parsley and serve immediately with grated Parmesan cheese.

Try This: FOR AN ALTERNATIVE: 84   FOR A DIFFERENT MEAT OPTION: 116

Swedish Cocktail Meatballs

SERVES 4–6

50 g/2 oz butter
1 onion, peeled and
    finely chopped
50 g/2 oz fresh white
    breadcrumbs
1 medium egg, beaten

125 ml/4 fl oz double cream
salt and freshly ground
    black pepper
350 g/12 oz fresh lean
    beef mince
125 g/4 oz fresh pork mince

3–4 tbsp freshly chopped dill
½ tsp ground allspice
1 tbsp vegetable oil
125 ml/4 fl oz beef stock
cream cheese and chive or
    cranberry sauce, to serve

Heat half the butter in a large wok, add the onion and cook, stirring frequently, for 4–6 minutes, or until softened and beginning to colour. Transfer to a bowl and leave to cool. Wipe out the wok with absorbent kitchen paper.

Add the breadcrumbs and beaten egg with 1–2 tablespoons of cream to the softened onion. Season to taste with salt and pepper and stir until well blended. Using your fingertips crumble the beef and pork mince into the bowl. Add half the dill, the allspice and, using your hands, mix together until well blended. With dampened hands, shape the mixture into 2.5 cm/ 1 inch balls.

Melt the remaining butter in the wok and add the vegetable oil, swirling it to coat the side of the wok. Working in batches, add about one quarter to one third of the meatballs in a single layer and cook for 5 minutes, swirling and turning until golden and cooked. Transfer to a plate and continue with the remaining meatballs, transferring them to the plate as they are cooked.

Pour off the fat in the wok. Add the beef stock and bring to the boil, then boil until reduced by half, stirring and scraping up any browned bits from the bottom. Add the remaining cream and continue to simmer until slightly thickened and reduced. Stir in the remaining dill and season if necessary. Add the meatballs and simmer for 2–3 minutes, or until heated right through. Serve with cocktail sticks, with the sauce in a separate bowl for dipping.

Try This: FOR AN ALTERNATIVE: 82   FOR A DIFFERENT MEAT OPTION: 170

Meatballs with Bean & Tomato Sauce

SERVES 4

1 large onion, peeled and finely chopped
1 red pepper, deseeded and chopped
1 tbsp freshly chopped oregano
½ tsp hot paprika
425 g can red kidney beans, drained
300 g/11 oz fresh beef mince
salt and freshly ground black pepper
4 tbsp sunflower oil
1 garlic clove, peeled
and crushed
400 g can chopped tomatoes
1 tbsp freshly chopped coriander, to garnish
freshly cooked rice, to serve

Make the meatballs by blending half the onion, half the red pepper, the oregano, the paprika and 350 g/12 oz of the kidney beans in a blender or food processor for a few seconds. Add the beef with seasoning and blend until well mixed. Turn the mixture on to a lightly floured board and form into small balls.

Heat the wok, then add 2 tablespoons of the oil and, when hot, stir-fry the meatballs gently until well browned on all sides. Remove with a slotted spoon and keep warm.

Wipe the wok clean, then add the remaining oil and cook the remaining onion and pepper and the garlic for 3–4 minutes, until soft. Add the tomatoes, seasoning to taste and remaining kidney beans.

Return the meatballs to the wok, stir them into the sauce, then cover and simmer for 10 minutes. Sprinkle with the chopped coriander and serve immediately with the freshly cooked rice.

Try This: FOR AN ALTERNATIVE: 82   FOR A DIFFERENT MEAT OPTION: 190

Italian Meatballs in Tomato Sauce

SERVES 4

For the tomato sauce:
4 tbsp olive oil
1 large onion, peeled and
    finely chopped
2 garlic cloves, peeled
    and chopped
400 g can chopped tomatoes
1 tbsp sun-dried tomato paste

1 tbsp dried mixed herbs
150 ml/¼ pint red wine
salt and freshly ground
    black pepper

For the meatballs:
450 g/1 lb fresh pork mince
50 g/2 oz fresh breadcrumbs

1 medium egg yolk
75 g/3 oz Parmesan
    cheese, grated
20 small stuffed green olives
freshly snipped chives,
    to garnish
freshly cooked pasta, to serve

To make the tomato sauce, heat half the olive oil in a saucepan and cook half the chopped onion for 5 minutes, until softened. Add the garlic, chopped tomatoes, tomato paste, mixed herbs and red wine to the pan and season to taste with salt and pepper. Stir well until blended. Bring to the boil, then cover and simmer for 15 minutes.

To make the meatballs, place the pork, breadcrumbs, remaining onion, egg yolk and half the Parmesan in a large bowl. Season well and mix together with your hands. Divide the mixture into 20 balls.

Flatten 1 ball out in the palm of your hands, place an olive in the centre, then squeeze the meat around the olive to enclose completely. Repeat with remaining mixture and olives. Place the meatballs on a baking sheet and cover with clingfilm and chill in the refrigerator for 30 minutes.

Heat the remaining oil in a large frying pan and cook the meatballs for 8–10 minutes, turning occasionally, until golden brown. Pour in the sauce and heat through. Sprinkle with chives and the remaining Parmesan. Serve immediately with the freshly cooked pasta.

Try This: FOR AN ALTERNATIVE: 80   FOR A DIFFERENT MEAT OPTION: 116

Spaghetti & Meatballs

SERVES 4

400 g can chopped tomatoes
1 tbsp tomato paste
1 tsp chilli sauce
¼ tsp brown sugar
salt and freshly ground
    black pepper
350 g/12 oz spaghetti
75g/3 oz Cheddar cheese,
    grated, plus extra to serve

freshly chopped parsley,
    to garnish

For the meatballs:
450 g/1 lb lean pork or
    beef mince
125 g/4 oz
    fresh breadcrumbs
1 large onion, peeled and

finely chopped
1 medium egg, beaten
1 tbsp tomato paste
2 tbsp freshly chopped
    parsley
1 tbsp freshly
    chopped oregano

Preheat the oven to 200°C/400°F/Gas Mark 6, 15 minutes before using. Place the chopped tomatoes, tomato paste, chilli sauce and sugar in a saucepan. Season to taste with salt and pepper and bring to the boil. Cover and simmer for 15 minutes, then cook, uncovered, for a further 10 minutes, or until the sauce has reduced and thickened.

Meanwhile, make the meatballs. Place the meat, breadcrumbs and onion in a food processor. Blend until all the ingredients are well mixed. Add the beaten egg, tomato paste, parsley and oregano and season to taste. Blend again. Shape the mixture into small balls, about the size of an apricot, and place on an oiled baking tray. Cook in the preheated oven for 25–30 minutes, or until browned and cooked.

Meanwhile, bring a large pan of lightly salted water to a rolling boil. Add the pasta and cook according to the packet instructions, or until 'al dente'.

Drain the pasta and return to the pan. Pour over the tomato sauce and toss gently to coat the spaghetti. Tip into a warmed serving dish and top with the meatballs. Garnish with chopped parsley and serve immediately with grated cheese.

 Try This: FOR AN ALTERNATIVE: 88   FOR A DIFFERENT MEAT OPTION: 276

Traditional Lasagne

SERVES 4

450 g/1 lb lean minced beef steak
175 g/6 oz pancetta or smoked streaky bacon, chopped
1 large onion, peeled and chopped
2 celery stalks, trimmed and chopped
125 g/4 oz button mushrooms, wiped and chopped

2 garlic cloves, peeled and chopped
90 g/3½ oz plain flour
300 ml/½ pint beef stock
1 tbsp freeze-dried mixed herbs
5 tbsp tomato purée
salt and freshly ground black pepper
75 g/3 oz butter
1 tsp English mustard powder

pinch of freshly grated nutmeg
900 ml/1½ pints milk
125 g/4 oz Parmesan cheese, grated
125 g/4 oz Cheddar cheese, grated
8–12 precooked lasagne sheets
crusty bread, to serve
fresh green salad leaves, to serve

Preheat the oven to 200°C/400°F/Gas Mark 6, 15 minutes before cooking. Cook the beef and pancetta in a large saucepan for 10 minutes, stirring to break up any lumps. Add the onion, celery and mushrooms and cook for 4 minutes, or until softened slightly. Stir in the garlic and 1 tablespoon of the flour, then cook for 1 minute. Stir in the stock, herbs and tomato purée. Season to taste with salt and pepper. Bring to the boil, then cover, reduce the heat and simmer for 45 minutes.

Meanwhile, melt the butter in a small saucepan and stir in the remaining flour, mustard powder and nutmeg, until well blended. Cook for 2 minutes. Remove from the heat and gradually blend in the milk until smooth. Return to the heat and bring to the boil, stirring, until thickened. Gradually stir in half the Parmesan and Cheddar cheeses until melted. Season to taste.

Spoon half the meat mixture into the base of a large ovenproof dish. Top with a single layer of pasta. Spread over half the sauce and scatter with half the cheese. Repeat layers finishing with cheese. Bake in the preheated oven for 30 minutes, or until the pasta is cooked and the top is golden brown and bubbly. Serve immediately with crusty bread and a green salad.

Try This: FOR AN ALTERNATIVE: 88   FOR A DIFFERENT MEAT OPTION: 134

Spaghetti Bolognese

SERVES 4

3 tbsp olive oil
50 g/2 oz unsmoked streaky
   bacon, rind removed
   and chopped
1 small onion, peeled
   and finely chopped
1 carrot, peeled and
   finely chopped

1 celery stalk, trimmed and
   finely chopped
2 garlic cloves, peeled
   and crushed
1 bay leaf
500 g/1 lb 2 oz minced
   beef steak
400 g can chopped tomatoes

2 tbsp tomato paste
150 ml/¼ pint red wine
150 ml/1/4 pint beef stock
salt and freshly gound
   black pepper
450 g/1 lb spaghetti
freshly grated Parmesan
   cheese, to serve

Heat the olive oil in a large heavy-based pan, add the bacon and cook for 5 minutes or until slightly coloured. Add the onion, carrot, celery, garlic and bay leaf and cook, stirring, for 8 minutes, or until the vegetables are soft.

Add the minced beef to the pan and cook, stirring with a wooden spoon to break up any lumps in the meat, for 5-8 minutes, or until browned.

Stir the tomatoes and tomato paste into the mince and pour in the wine and stock. Bring to the boil, lower the heat and simmer for at least 40 minutes, stirring occasionally. The longer you leave the sauce to cook, the more intense the flavour. Season to taste with salt and pepper and remove the bay leaf.

Meanwhile, bring a large pan of lightly salted water to a rolling boil, add the spaghetti and cook for about 8 minutes or until 'al dente'. Drain and arrange on warmed serving plates. Top with the prepared Bolognese sauce and serve immediately sprinkled with grated Parmesan cheese.

  Try This: FOR AN ALTERNATIVE: 86 FOR A DIFFERENT MEAT OPTION: 238

Cannelloni with Spicy Bolognese Filling

SERVES 6

12 dried cannelloni tubes
300 ml/½ pint double cream
75 g/3 oz freshly grated
    Parmesan cheese
¼ tsp freshly grated nutmeg
crisp green salad, to serve

Spicy Bolognese filling:
2 tbsp olive oil
1 small onion, peeled
    and finely chopped
2 garlic cloves, peeled
    and crushed
500 g/1 lb 2 oz minced
    beef steak
¼ tsp crushed chilli flakes

1 tsp fennel seeds
2 tbsp freshly
    chopped oregano
400 g can chopped tomatoes
1 tbsp sun-dried tomato paste
150 ml/¼ pint red wine
salt and freshly ground
    black pepper

Preheat the oven to 200°C/400°F/Gas Mark 6, 15 minutes before cooking the stuffed cannelloni. To make the Bolognese sauce, heat the oil in a large heavy-based pan, add the onion and garlic and cook for 8 minutes, or until soft. Add the minced beef and cook, stirring with a wooden spoon to break up lumps, for 5–8 minutes, or until the meat is browned.

Stir in the chilli flakes, fennel seeds, oregano, tomatoes and tomato paste and pour in the wine. Season well with salt and pepper. Bring to the boil, cover and lower the heat, then simmer for at least 30 minutes, stirring occasionally. Remove the lid and simmer for a further 10 minutes. Allow to cool slightly.

Using a teaspoon, fill the cannelloni tubes with the meat filling. Lay the stuffed cannelloni side by side in a lightly oiled ovenproof dish.

Mix the double cream with three-quarters of the Parmesan cheese and the nutmeg. Pour over the cannelloni and sprinkle with the remaining cheese. Bake in the preheated oven for 30 minutes, or until golden brown and bubbling. Serve immediately with a green salad.

Try This: FOR AN ALTERNATIVE: 82   FOR A DIFFERENT MEAT OPTION: 266

Fillet Steaks with Tomato & Garlic Sauce

SERVES 4

700 g/1½ lb ripe tomatoes
2 garlic cloves
2 tbsp olive oil
2 tbsp freshly chopped basil
2 tbsp freshly

chopped oregano
2 tbsp red wine
salt and freshly ground
black pepper
75 g/3 oz pitted black

olives, chopped
4 fillet steaks, about 175 g/6
oz each in weight
freshly cooked vegetables,
to serve

Make a small cross on the top of each tomato and place in a large bowl. Cover with boiling water and leave for 2 minutes. Using a slotted spoon, remove the tomatoes and skin carefully. Repeat until all the tomatoes are skinned. Place on a chopping board, cut into quarters, remove the seeds and roughly chop, then reserve.

Peel and chop the garlic. Heat half the olive oil in a saucepan and cook the garlic for 30 seconds. Add the chopped tomatoes with the basil, oregano, red wine and season to taste with salt and pepper. Bring to the boil then reduce the heat, cover and simmer for 15 minutes, stirring occasionally, or until the sauce is reduced and thickened. Stir the olives into the sauce and keep warm while cooking the steaks.

Meanwhile, lightly oil a griddle pan or heavy-based frying pan with the remaining olive oil and cook the steaks for 2 minutes on each side to seal. Continue to cook the steaks for a further 2–4 minutes, depending on personal preference. Serve the steaks immediately with the garlic sauce and freshly cooked vegetables.

Try This: FOR AN ALTERNATIVE: 66   FOR A DIFFERENT MEAT OPTION: 148

Veal Escalopes with Marsala Sauce

SERVES 6

6 veal escalopes, about
   125 g/4 oz each
lemon juice
salt and freshly ground
   black pepper
6 sage leaves

6 slices prosciutto
2 tbsp olive oil
25 g/1 oz butter
1 onion, peeled and sliced
1 garlic clove, peeled
   and chopped

2 tbsp Marsala wine
4 tbsp double cream
2 tbsp freshly chopped parsley
sage leaves to garnish
selection of freshly cooked
   vegetables, to serve

Place the veal escalopes between sheets of non-pvc clingfilm and using a mallet or rolling pin, pound lightly to flatten out thinly to about 5 mm/¼ inch thickness. Remove the clingfilm and sprinkle the veal escalopes with lemon juice, salt and black pepper.

Place a sage leaf in the centre of each escalope. Top with a slice of prosciutto making sure it just fits, then roll up the escalopes enclosing the prosciutto and sage leaves. Secure each escalope with a cocktail stick.

Heat the olive oil and butter in a large non-stick frying pan and fry the onions for 5 minutes, or until softened. Add the garlic and rolled escalopes and cook for about 8 minutes, turning occasionally, until the escalopes are browned all over.

Add the Marsala wine and cream to the pan and bring to the boil, cover and simmer for 10 minutes, or until the veal is tender. Season to taste and then sprinkle with the parsley. Discard the cocktail sticks and serve immediately with a selection of freshly cooked vegetables.

Try This: FOR AN ALTERNATIVE: 96 FOR A DIFFERENT MEAT OPTION: 252

Vitello Tonnato
(Veal in Tuna Sauce)

SERVES 6–8

900g/2 lb boned, rolled leg
   or loin of veal
300 ml/½ pint dry white wine
1 onion, peeled and chopped
1 carrot, peeled and chopped
2 celery stalks, trimmed
   and chopped
1 bay leaf
2 garlic cloves

few sprigs of parsley
salt and freshly ground
   black pepper
200 g can tuna in oil
2 tbsp capers, drained
6 anchovy fillets
200 ml/7 fl oz mayonnaise
juice of ½ lemon

To garnish:
lemon wedges
capers
black olives

To serve:
fresh green salad leaves
tomato wedges

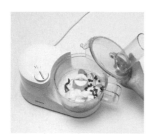

Place the veal in a large bowl and pour over the wine. Add the onion, carrot, celery, bay leaf, garlic cloves, parsley, salt and pepper. Cover tightly and chill overnight in the refrigerator. Transfer the contents of the bowl to a large saucepan, add just enough water to cover the meat. Bring to the boil, cover and simmer for 1–1¼ hours, or until the veal is tender.

Remove from the heat and allow the veal to cool in the juices. Using a slotted spoon, transfer the veal to a plate, pat dry with absorbent kitchen paper and reserve.

Place the tuna, capers, anchovy fillets, mayonnaise and lemon juice in a food processor or liquidiser and blend until smooth, adding a few spoonfuls of the pan juices to make the sauce of a coating consistency, if necessary. Season to taste with salt and pepper.

Using a sharp knife slice the veal thinly and arrange on a large serving platter.

Spoon the sauce over the veal. Cover with clingfilm and chill in the refrigerator overnight. Garnish with lemon wedges, capers and olives. Serve with salad and tomato wedges.

Try This: FOR AN ALTERNATIVE: 94 FOR A DIFFERENT MEAT OPTION: 122

Italian Beef Pot Roast

SERVES 6

1.8 kg/4 lb brisket of beef
225 g/8 oz small onions,
    peeled
3 garlic cloves, peeled
    and chopped
2 celery sticks, trimmed
    and chopped

2 carrots, peeled and sliced
450 g/1 lb ripe tomatoes
300 ml/½ pint Italian red wine
2 tbsp olive oil
300 ml/½ pint beef stock
1 tbsp tomato purée
2 tsp freeze-dried mixed herbs

salt and freshly ground
    black pepper
25 g/1 oz butter
25 g/1 oz plain flour
freshly cooked vegetables,
    to serve

Preheat oven to 150°C/300°F/Gas Mark 2, 10 minutes before cooking. Place the beef in a bowl. Add the onions, garlic, celery and carrots. Place the tomatoes in a bowl and cover with boiling water. Allow to stand for 2 minutes and drain. Peel away the skins, discard the seeds and chop, then add to the bowl with the red wine. Cover tightly and marinate in the refrigerator overnight.

Lift the marinated beef from the bowl and pat dry with absorbent kitchen paper. Heat the olive oil in a large casserole and cook the beef until it is browned all over, then remove from the dish. Drain the vegetables from the marinade, reserving the marinade. Add the vegetables to the casserole and fry gently for 5 minutes, stirring occasionally, until all the vegetables are browned.

Return the beef to the casserole with the marinade, beef stock, tomato purée and mixed herbs and season with salt and pepper. Bring to the boil, then cover and cook in the preheated oven for 3 hours.

Using a slotted spoon transfer the beef and any large vegetables to a plate and leave in a warm place. Blend the butter and flour to form a paste. Bring the casserole juices to the boil and then gradually stir in small spoonfuls of the paste. Cook until thickened. Serve with the sauce and a selection of vegetables.

Try This: FOR AN ALTERNATIVE: 108   FOR A DIFFERENT MEAT OPTION: 120

Italian Calf Liver

SERVES 4

450 g/1 lb calf liver, trimmed
1 onion, peeled and sliced
2 fresh bay leaves,
    coarsely torn
fresh parsley sprigs
fresh sage leaves
5 black peppercorns,
    lightly crushed
1 tbsp redcurrant

jelly, warmed
4 tbsp walnut or olive oil
4 tbsp red wine vinegar
3 tbsp plain white flour
salt and freshly ground
    black pepper
2 garlic cloves, peeled
    and crushed
1 red pepper, deseeded

and sliced
1 yellow pepper, deseeded
    and sliced
3 tbsp sun-dried tomatoes,
    chopped
150 ml/¼ pint chicken stock
fresh sage leaves, to garnish
diced sauté potatoes, to serve

Cut the liver into very thin slices and place in a shallow dish. Sprinkle over the onion, bay leaves, parsley, sage and peppercorns. Blend the redcurrant jelly with 1 tablespoon of the oil and the vinegar. Pour over the liver, cover and leave to marinate for at least 30 minutes. Turn the liver occasionally or spoon over the marinade.

Remove the liver from the marinade, strain the liquor and reserve. Season the flour with salt and pepper, then use to coat the liver. Add the remaining oil to a heavy-based frying pan, then sauté the garlic and peppers for 5 minutes. Using a slotted spoon, remove from the pan.

Add the liver to the pan, turn the heat up to high and cook until the meat is browned on all sides. Return the garlic and peppers to the pan and add the reserved marinade, the sun-dried tomatoes and stock. Bring to the boil, then reduce the heat and simmer for 3–4 minutes, or until the liver is cooked. Add more seasoning, then garnish with a few sage leaves and serve immediately with diced sauté potatoes.

Try This: FOR AN ALTERNATIVE: 72 FOR A DIFFERENT MEAT OPTION: 114

Spicy Chilli Beef

SERVES 4

2 tbsp olive oil
1 onion, peeled and
   finely chopped
1 red pepper, deseeded
   and sliced
450 g/1 lb minced beef steak
2 garlic cloves, peeled
   and crushed

2 red chillies, deseeded
   and finely sliced
salt and freshly ground
   black pepper
400 g can chopped tomatoes
2 tbsp tomato paste
400 g can red kidney
   beans, drained

50 g/2 oz good quality, plain
   dark chocolate, grated
350 g/12 oz dried fusilli
knob of butter
2 tbsp freshly chopped
   flat-leaf parsley
paprika, to garnish
soured cream, to serve

Heat the olive oil in a large heavy-based pan. Add the onion and red pepper and cook for 5 minutes, or until beginning to soften. Add the minced beef and cook over a high heat for 5–8 minutes, or until the meat is browned. Stir with a wooden spoon during cooking to break up any lumps in the meat. Add the garlic and chilli, fry for 1 minute then season to taste with salt and pepper.

Add the chopped tomatoes, tomato paste and the kidney beans to the pan. Bring to the boil, lower the heat, and simmer, covered, for at least 40 minutes, stirring occasionally. Stir in the grated chocolate and cook for 3 minutes, or until melted.

Meanwhile, bring a large pan of lightly salted water to a rolling boil. Add the fusilli and cook according to the packet instructions, or until 'al dente'.

Drain the pasta, return to the pan and toss with the butter and parsley. Tip into a warmed serving dish or spoon on to individual plates. Spoon the sauce over the pasta. Sprinkle with paprika and serve immediately with spoonfuls of soured cream.

Try This: FOR AN ALTERNATIVE: 58   FOR A DIFFERENT MEAT OPTION: 124

Pasta with Beef, Capers & Olives

SERVES 4

2 tbsp olive oil
300 g/11 oz rump steak,
    trimmed and cut into strips
4 spring onions, trimmed
    and sliced
2 garlic cloves, peeled
    and chopped
2 courgettes, trimmed

and cut into strips
1 red pepper, deseeded and
    cut into strips
2 tsp freshly chopped oregano
2 tbsp capers, drained
    and rinsed
4 tbsp pitted black
    olives, sliced

400 g can chopped tomatoes
salt and freshly ground
    black pepper
450 g/1 lb fettuccine
1 tbsp freshly chopped
    parsley, to garnish

Heat the olive oil in a large frying pan over a high heat. Add the steak and cook, stirring, for 3–4 minutes, or until browned. Remove from the pan using a slotted spoon and reserve.

Lower the heat, add the spring onions and garlic to the pan and cook for 1 minute. Add the courgettes and pepper and cook for 3–4 minutes.

Add the oregano, capers and olives to the pan with the chopped tomatoes. Season to taste with salt and pepper, then simmer for 7 minutes, stirring occasionally. Return the beef to the pan and simmer for 3–5 minutes, or until the sauce has thickened slightly.

Meanwhile, bring a large pan of lightly salted water to a rolling boil. Add the pasta and cook according to the packet instructions, or until 'al dente'.

Drain the pasta thoroughly. Return to the pan and add the beef sauce. Toss gently until the pasta is lightly coated. Tip into a warmed serving dish or on to individual plates. Sprinkle with chopped parsley and serve immediately.

Try This: FOR AN ALTERNATIVE: 74 FOR A DIFFERENT MEAT OPTION: 160

Chinese Beef with Angel Hair Pasta

SERVES 4

1 tbsp pink peppercorns
1 tbsp chilli powder
1 tbsp Szechuan pepper
3 tbsp light soy sauce
3 tbsp dry sherry
450 g/1 lb sirloin steak,
   cut into strips

350 g/12 oz angel hair pasta
1 tbsp sesame oil
1 tbsp sunflower oil
1 bunch spring onions,
   trimmed and finely
   shredded, plus extra
   to garnish

1 red pepper, deseeded
   and thinly sliced
1 green pepper, deseeded
   and thinly sliced
1 tbsp toasted sesame
   seeds, to garnish

Crush the peppercorns, using a pestle and mortar. Transfer to a shallow bowl and combine with the chilli powder, Szechuan pepper, light soy sauce and sherry. Add the beef strips and stir until lightly coated. Cover and place in the refrigerator to marinate for 3 hours; stir occasionally during this time.

When ready to cook, bring a large pan of lightly salted water to a rolling boil. Add the pasta and cook according to the packet instructions, or until 'al dente'. Drain thoroughly and return to the pan. Add the sesame oil and toss lightly. Keep the pasta warm.

Heat a wok or large frying pan, add the sunflower oil and heat until very hot. Add the shredded spring onions with the sliced red and green peppers and stir-fry for 2 minutes.

Drain the beef, reserving the marinade, then add the beef to the wok or pan and stir-fry for 3 minutes. Pour the marinade and stir-fry for 1-2 minutes, until the steak is tender.

Pile the pasta on to 4 warmed plates. Top with the stir-fried beef and peppers and garnish with toasted sesame seeds and shredded spring onions. Serve immediately.

Try This: FOR AN ALTERNATIVE: 26 FOR A DIFFERENT MEAT OPTION: 280

Gnocchi with Tuscan Beef Ragù

SERVES 4

25 g/1 oz dried porcini
3 tbsp olive oil
1 small onion, peeled
and finely chopped
1 carrot, peeled and
finely chopped
1 celery, trimmed and
finely chopped
1 fennel bulb, trimmed
and sliced
2 garlic cloves, peeled
and crushed
450 g/1 lb fresh beef
steak mince
4 tbsp red wine
50 g/2 oz pine nuts
1 tbsp freshly
chopped rosemary
2 tbsp tomato paste
400 g can chopped tomatoes
225 g/8 oz fresh gnocchi
salt and freshly ground
black pepper
100 g/4 oz mozzarella
cheese, cubed

Preheat the oven to 200°C/400°F/Gas Mark 6, 15 minutes before cooking. Place the porcini in a small bowl and cover with almost boiling water. Leave to soak for 30 minutes. Drain, reserving the soaking liquid and straining it through a muslin-lined sieve. Chop the porcini.

Heat the olive oil in a large heavy-based pan. Add the onion, carrot, celery, fennel and garlic and cook for 8 minutes, stirring, or until soft. Add the minced steak and cook, stirring, for 5–8 minutes, or until sealed and any lumps are broken up. Pour in the wine, then add the porcini with half the pine nuts, the rosemary and tomato paste. Stir in the porcini soaking liquid then simmer for 5 minutes. Add the chopped tomatoes and simmer gently for about 40 minutes, stirring occasionally.

Meanwhile, bring 1.7 litres/3 pints of lightly salted water to a rolling boil in a large pan. Add the gnocchi and cook for 1–2 minutes, until they rise to the surface.

Drain the gnocchi and place in an ovenproof dish. Stir in three-quarters of the mozzarella cheese with the beef sauce. Top with the remaining mozzarella and pine nuts, then bake in the preheated oven for 20 minutes, until golden brown. Serve immediately.

Try This: FOR AN ALTERNATIVE: 88 FOR A DIFFERENT MEAT OPTION: 278

Lamb

Kung–pao Lamb

SERVES 4

450 g/1 lb lamb fillet
2 tbsp soy sauce
2 tbsp Chinese rice wine
  or dry sherry
2 tbsp sunflower oil
2 tsp sesame oil
50 g/2 oz unsalted peanuts
1 garlic clove, peeled
  and crushed

2.5 cm/1 inch piece fresh
  root ginger,
  finely chopped
1 red chilli, deseeded and
  finely chopped
1 small green pepper,
  deseeded and diced
6 spring onions, trimmed
  and diagonally sliced

125 ml/4 fl oz lamb
  or vegetable stock
1 tsp red wine vinegar
1 tsp soft light brown sugar
2 tsp cornflour
plain boiled or steamed
  white rice, to serve

Wrap the lamb in baking parchment paper and place in the freezer for about 30 minutes until stiff. Cut the meat across the grain into paper-thin slices. Put in a shallow bowl, add 2 teaspoons of the soy sauce and all the Chinese rice wine or sherry and leave to marinate in the refrigerator for 15 minutes.

Heat a wok or frying pan until hot, add the sunflower oil and swirl it around to coat the sides. Add the lamb and stir-fry for about 1 minute until lightly browned. Remove from the wok or pan and reserve, leaving any juices behind.

Add the sesame oil to the wok or pan and stir-fry the peanuts, garlic, ginger, chilli, green pepper and spring onions for 1–2 minutes, or until the nuts are golden. Return the lamb with the remaining soy sauce, stock, vinegar and sugar.

Blend the cornflour with 1 tablespoon of water. Stir in and cook the mixture for 1–2 minutes, or until the vegetables are tender and the sauce has thickened. Serve immediately with plain boiled or steamed white rice.

Try This: FOR AN ALTERNATIVE: 138   FOR A DIFFERENT MEAT OPTION: 40

Lamb with Stir-fried Vegetables

SERVES 4

550 g/1¼ lb lamb fillet, cut into strips
2.5 cm/1 inch piece fresh root ginger, peeled and cut into matchsticks
2 garlic cloves, peeled and chopped
4 tbsp soy sauce
2 tbsp dry sherry

2 tsp cornflour
4 tbsp groundnut oil
75 g/3 oz French beans, trimmed and cut in half
2 medium carrots, peeled and cut into matchsticks
1 red pepper, deseeded and cut into chunks
1 yellow pepper, deseeded

and cut into chunks
225 g can water chestnuts, drained and halved
3 tomatoes, chopped
freshly cooked sticky rice in banana leaves, to serve (optional)

Place the lamb strips in a shallow dish. Mix together the ginger and half the garlic in a small bowl. Pour over the soy sauce and sherry and stir well. Pour over the lamb and stir until coated lightly. Cover with clingfilm and leave to marinate for at least 30 minutes, occasionally spooning the marinade over the lamb.

Using a slotted spoon, lift the lamb from the marinade and place on a plate. Blend the cornflour and the marinade together until smooth and reserve.

Heat a wok or large frying pan, add 2 tablespoons of the oil and when hot, add the remaining garlic, French beans, carrots and peppers and stir-fry for 5 minutes. Using a slotted spoon, transfer the vegetables to a plate and keep warm.

Heat the remaining oil in the wok, add the lamb and stir-fry for 2 minutes or until tender. Return the vegetables to the wok with the water chestnuts, tomatoes and reserved marinade mixture. Bring to the boil then simmer for 1 minute. Serve immediately with freshly cooked sticky rice in banana leaves, if liked.

Try This: FOR AN ALTERNATIVE: 156 FOR A DIFFERENT MEAT OPTION: 48

Lamb Meatballs
with Savoy Cabbage

SERVES 4

450 g/1 lb fresh lamb mince
1 tbsp freshly chopped parsley
1 tbsp freshly grated
   root ginger
1 tbsp light soy sauce
1 medium egg yolk
4 tbsp dark soy sauce

2 tbsp dry sherry
1 tbsp cornflour
3 tbsp vegetable oil
2 garlic cloves, peeled and
   chopped
1 bunch spring onions,
   trimmed and shredded

½ Savoy cabbage, trimmed
   and shredded
½ head Chinese leaves,
   trimmed and shredded
freshly chopped red chilli,
   to garnish

Place the lamb mince in a large bowl with the parsley, ginger, light soy sauce and egg yolk and mix together. Divide the mixture into walnut-sized pieces and using your hands roll into balls. Place on a baking sheet, cover with clingfilm and chill in the refrigerator for at least 30 minutes.

Meanwhile, blend together the dark soy sauce, sherry and cornflour with 2 tablespoons of water in a small bowl until smooth. Reserve.

Heat a wok, add the oil and when hot, add the meatballs and cook for 5–8 minutes, or until browned all over, turning occasionally. Using a slotted spoon, transfer the meatballs to a large plate and keep warm.

Add the garlic, spring onions, Savoy cabbage and the Chinese leaves to the wok and stir-fry for 3 minutes. Pour over the reserved soy sauce mixture, bring to the boil, then simmer for 30 seconds or until thickened. Return the meatballs to the wok and mix in. Garnish with chopped red chilli and serve immediately.

Try This: FOR AN ALTERNATIVE: 112 FOR A DIFFERENT MEAT OPTION: 190

Spicy Lamb & Peppers

SERVES 4

550 g/1¼ lb lamb fillet
4 tbsp soy sauce
1 tbsp dry sherry
1 tbsp cornflour
3 tbsp vegetable oil
1 bunch spring
 onions, shredded
225 g/8 oz broccoli florets
2 garlic cloves, peeled

and chopped
2.5 cm/1 inch piece fresh
 root ginger, peeled and
 cut into matchsticks
1 red pepper, deseeded and
 cut into chunks
1 green pepper, deseeded
 and cut into chunks
2 tsp Chinese five-

spice powder
1–2 tsp dried crushed
 chillies, or to taste
1 tbsp tomato purée
1 tbsp rice wine vinegar
1 tbsp soft brown sugar
freshly cooked noodles,
 to serve

Cut the lamb into 2 cm/¾ inch slices, then place in a shallow dish. Blend the soy sauce, sherry and cornflour together in a small bowl and pour over the lamb. Turn the lamb until coated lightly with the marinade. Cover with clingfilm and leave to marinate in the refrigerator for at least 30 minutes, turning occasionally.

Heat a wok or large frying pan, add the oil and when hot, stir-fry the spring onions and broccoli for 2 minutes. Add the garlic, ginger and peppers and stir-fry for a further 2 minutes. Using a slotted spoon, transfer the vegetables to a plate and keep warm.

Using a slotted spoon, lift the lamb from the marinade, shaking off any excess marinade. Add to the wok and stir-fry for 5 minutes, or until browned all over. Reserve the marinade.

Return the vegetables to the wok and stir in the Chinese five-spice powder, chillies, tomato purée, reserved marinade, vinegar and sugar. Bring to the boil, stirring constantly, until thickened. Simmer for 2 minutes or until heated through thoroughly. Serve immediately with noodles.

Try This: FOR AN ALTERNATIVE: 126 FOR A DIFFERENT MEAT OPTION: 192

Brandied Lamb Chops

SERVES 4

8 lamb loin chops
3 tbsp groundnut oil
5 cm/2 inch piece fresh root
   ginger, peeled and cut
   into matchsticks
2 garlic cloves, peeled
   and chopped
225 g/8 oz button mushrooms,

   wiped, and halved if large
2 tbsp light soy sauce
2 tbsp dry sherry
1 tbsp brandy
1 tsp Chinese five-
   spice powder
1 tsp soft brown sugar
200 ml/7 fl oz lamb or

   chicken stock
1 tsp sesame oil

To serve:
freshly cooked rice
freshly stir-fried vegetables

Using a sharp knife, trim the lamb chops, discarding any sinew or fat. Heat a wok or large frying pan, add the oil and when hot, add the lamb chops and cook for 3 minutes on each side or until browned. Using a fish slice, transfer the lamb chops to a plate and keep warm.

Add the ginger, garlic and button mushrooms to the wok and stir-fry for 3 minutes or until the mushrooms have browned.

Return the lamb chops to the wok together with the soy sauce, sherry, brandy, five-spice powder and sugar. Pour in the stock, bring to the boil, then reduce the heat slightly and simmer for 4–5 minutes, or until the lamb is tender, ensuring that the liquid does not evaporate completely. Add the sesame oil and heat for a further 30 seconds. Turn into a warmed serving dish and serve immediately with freshly cooked rice and stir-fried vegetables.

Try This: FOR AN ALTERNATIVE: 148   FOR A DIFFERENT MEAT OPTION: 42

Lamb with Black Cherry Sauce

SERVES 4

550 g/1¼ lb lamb fillet
2 tbsp light soy sauce
1 tsp Chinese five-
    spice powder
4 tbsp fresh orange juice
175 g/6 oz black cherry jam

150 ml/¼ pint red wine
50 g/2 oz fresh black cherries
1 tbsp groundnut oil
1 tbsp freshly chopped
    coriander, to garnish

To serve:
thawed frozen peas
freshly cooked noodles

Remove the skin and any fat from the lamb fillet and cut into thin slices. Place in a shallow dish. Mix together the soy sauce, Chinese five-spice powder and orange juice and pour over the meat. Cover and leave in the refrigerator for at least 30 minutes.

Meanwhile, blend the jam and the wine together, pour into a small saucepan and bring to the boil. Simmer gently for 10 minutes until slightly thickened. Remove the stones from the cherries, using a cherry stoner if possible in order to keep them whole.

Drain the lamb when ready to cook. Heat the wok, add the oil and when the oil is hot, stir-fry the slices of lamb for 3–5 minutes, or until just slightly pink inside or cooked to personal preference.

Spoon the lamb into a warm serving dish and serve immediately with a little of the cherry sauce drizzled over. Garnish with the chopped coriander and the whole cherries and serve immediately with peas, freshly cooked noodles and the remaining sauce.

Try This: FOR AN ALTERNATIVE: ??, ??, ??   FOR A DIFFERENT MEAT OPTION: ??, ??, ??

Chilli Lamb

SERVES 4

550 g/1¼ lb lamb fillet
3 tbsp groundnut oil
1 large onion, peeled
   and finely sliced
2 garlic cloves, peeled
   and crushed

4 tsp cornflour
4 tbsp hot chilli sauce
2 tbsp white wine vinegar
4 tsp dark soft brown sugar
1 tsp Chinese five-
   spice powder

sprigs of fresh coriander,
   to garnish

To serve:
freshly cooked noodles
4 tbsp Greek style yoghurt

Trim the lamb fillet, discarding any fat or sinew, then place it on a clean chopping board and cut into thin strips. Heat a wok and pour in 2 tablespoons of the groundnut oil and when hot, stir-fry the lamb for 3–4 minutes, or until it is browned. Remove the lamb strips with their juices and reserve.

Add the remaining oil to the wok, then stir-fry the onion and garlic for 2 minutes, or until softened. Remove with a slotted spoon and add to the lamb.

Blend the cornflour with 125 ml/4 fl oz of cold water, then stir in the chilli sauce, vinegar, sugar and Chinese five-spice powder. Pour this into the wok, turn up the heat and bring the mixture to the boil. Cook for 30 seconds or until the sauce thickens.

Return the lamb to the wok with the onion and garlic, stir thoroughly and heat through until piping hot. Garnish with sprigs of fresh coriander and serve immediately with freshly cooked noodles, topped with a spoonful of Greek yoghurt.

Try This: FOR AN ALTERNATIVE: 112 FOR A DIFFERENT MEAT OPTION: 32

Spicy Lamb in Yoghurt Sauce

SERVES 4

1 tsp hot chilli powder
1 tsp ground cinnamon
1 tsp medium hot
  curry powder
1 tsp ground cumin
salt and freshly ground
  black pepper
2 tbsp groundnut oil
450 g/1 lb lamb fillet, trimmed

4 cardamom pods, bruised
4 whole cloves
1 onion, peeled and
  finely sliced
2 garlic cloves, peeled
  and crushed
2.5 cm/1 inch piece fresh root
  ginger, peeled and grated
150 ml/¼ pint Greek

style yoghurt
1 tbsp freshly chopped
  coriander
2 spring onions, trimmed
  and finely sliced

To serve:
freshly cooked rice
naan bread

Blend the chilli powder, cinnamon, curry powder, cumin and seasoning with 2 tablespoons of the oil in a bowl and reserve. Cut the lamb fillet into thin strips, add to the spice and oil mixture and stir until coated thoroughly. Cover and leave to marinate in the refrigerator for at least 30 minutes.

Heat the wok, then pour in the remaining oil. When hot, add the cardamom pods and cloves and stir-fry for 10 seconds. Add the onion, garlic and ginger to the wok and stir-fry for 3–4 minutes until softened.

Add the lamb with the marinading ingredients and stir-fry for a further 3 minutes until cooked. Pour in the yoghurt, stir thoroughly and heat until piping hot. Sprinkle with the chopped coriander and sliced spring onions then serve immediately with freshly cooked rice and naan bread.

Try This: FOR AN ALTERNATIVE: 162   FOR A DIFFERENT MEAT OPTION: 74

Lamb's Liver
with Bacon & Onions

SERVES 4

350 g/12 oz lamb's liver
2 heaped tbsp plain flour
salt and freshly ground
   black pepper
2 tbsp groundnut oil
2 large onions, peeled
   and finely sliced
2 garlic cloves, peeled

and chopped
1 red chilli, deseeded
   and chopped
175 g/6 oz streaky bacon
40 g/1½ oz butter
300 ml/½ pint lamb
   or beef stock
2 tbsp freshly

chopped parsley

To serve:
freshly cooked creamy
   mashed potatoes
freshly cooked green
   vegetables
freshly cooked carrots

Trim the liver, discarding any sinew or tubes, and thinly slice. Season the flour with salt and pepper, then use to coat the liver and reserve.

Heat a wok, then add the oil and when hot, add the sliced onion, garlic and chilli and cook for 5–6 minutes, or until soft and browned. Remove from the wok with a slotted spoon and reserve. Cut each slice of the bacon in half and stir-fry for 3–4 minutes or until cooked. Remove with a slotted spoon and add to the onions.

Melt the butter in the wok and fry the liver on all sides until browned and crisp. Pour in the stock and allow to bubble fiercely for 1–2 minutes. Return the onions and bacon to the wok, stir thoroughly, then cover. Simmer gently for 10 minutes, or until the liver is tender. Sprinkle with the parsley and serve immediately with mashed potatoes and green vegetables and carrots.

Try This: FOR AN ALTERNATIVE: 146   FOR A DIFFERENT MEAT OPTION: 62

Moroccan Lamb with Apricots

SERVES 6

5 cm/2 inch piece root
   ginger, peeled and grated
3 garlic cloves, peeled
   and crushed
1 tsp ground cardamom
1 tsp ground cumin
2 tbsp olive oil

450 g/1 lb lamb neck
   fillet, cubed
1 large red onion, peeled
   and chopped
400 g can chopped tomatoes
125 g/4 oz ready-to-eat
   dried apricots

400 g can chickpeas, drained
7 large sheets filo pastry
50 g/2 oz butter, melted
pinch of nutmeg
dill sprigs, to garnish

Preheat the oven to 190°C/375°F/Gas Mark 5. Pound the ginger, garlic, cardamom and cumin to a paste with a pestle and mortar. Heat 1 tablespoon of the oil in a large frying pan and fry the spice paste for 3 minutes. Remove and reserve.

Add the remaining oil and fry the lamb in batches for about 5 minutes, until golden brown. Return all the lamb to the pan and add the onions and spice paste. Fry for 10 minutes, stirring occasionally. Add the chopped tomatoes, cover and simmer for 15 minutes. Add the apricots and chickpeas and simmer for a further 15 minutes.

Lightly oil a round 18 cm/7 inch spring form cake tin. Lay one sheet of filo pastry in the base of the tin, allowing the excess to fall over the sides. Brush with melted butter, then layer five more sheets in the tin, brushing each one with butter.

Spoon in the filling and level the surface. Layer half the remaining filo sheets on top, again brushing each with butter. Fold the overhanging pastry over the top of the filling. Brush the remaining sheet with butter and scrunch up and place on top of the pie so that the whole pie is completely covered. Brush with melted butter once more. Bake in the preheated oven for 45 minutes, then reserve for 10 minutes. Unclip the tin and remove the pie. Sprinkle with the nutmeg, garnish with the dill sprigs and serve.

Try This: FOR AN ALTERNATIVE: 122 FOR A DIFFERENT MEAT OPTION: 272

Leg of Lamb with Minted Rice

SERVES 4

1 tbsp olive oil
1 medium onion, peeled
 and finely chopped
1 garlic clove, peeled
 and crushed
1 celery stalk, trimmed
 and chopped
1 large mild red chilli,
 deseeded and chopped
75 g/3 oz long-grain rice
150 ml/¼ pint lamb or
 chicken stock
2 tbsp freshly chopped mint
salt and freshly ground
 black pepper
1.4 kg/3 lb boned leg of lamb
freshly cooked vegetables,
 to serve

Preheat the oven to 190°C/375°F/Gas Mark 5, 10 minutes before roasting. Heat the oil in a frying pan and gently cook the onion for 5 minutes. Stir in the garlic, celery and chilli and continue to cook for 3–4 minutes.

Place the rice and the stock in a large saucepan and cook, covered, for 10–12 minutes or until the rice is tender and all the liquid is absorbed. Stir in the onion and celery mixture, then leave to cool. Once the rice mixture is cold, stir in the chopped mint and season to taste with salt and pepper.

Place the boned lamb skin-side down and spoon the rice mixture along the centre of the meat. Roll up the meat to enclose the stuffing and tie securely with string. Place in a roasting tin and roast in the preheated oven for 1 hour 20 minutes, or until cooked to personal preference. Remove from the oven and leave to rest in a warm place for 20 minutes, before carving. Serve with a selection of cooked vegetables.

Try This: FOR AN ALTERNATIVE: 138 FOR A DIFFERENT MEAT OPTION: 236

Lamb & Potato Moussaka

SERVES 4

700 g/1½ lb cooked
   roast lamb
700 g/1½ lb potatoes, peeled
125 g/4 oz butter
1 large onion, peeled
   and chopped
2–4 garlic cloves, peeled

and crushed
3 tbsp tomato purée
1 tbsp freshly chopped parsley
salt and freshly ground
   black pepper
3–4 tbsp olive oil
2 medium aubergines,

trimmed and sliced
4 medium tomatoes, sliced
2 medium eggs
300 ml/½ pint Greek yoghurt
2–3 tbsp Parmesan cheese,
   grated

Preheat the oven to 200°C/400°F/Gas Mark 6, about 15 minutes before required. Trim the lamb, discarding any fat then cut into fine dice and reserve. Thinly slice the potatoes and rinse thoroughly in cold water, then pat dry with a clean tea towel.

Melt 50 g/2 oz of the butter in a frying pan and fry the potatoes, in batches, until crisp and golden. Using a slotted spoon, remove from the pan and reserve. Use a third of the potatoes to line the base of an ovenproof dish.

Add the onion and garlic to the butter remaining in the pan and cook for 5 minutes. Add the lamb and fry for 1 minute. Blend the tomato purée with 3 tablespoons of water and stir into the pan with the parsley and salt and pepper. Spoon over the layer of potatoes, then top with the remaining potato slices.

Heat the oil and the remaining butter in the pan and brown the aubergine slices for 5–6 minutes. Arrange the tomatoes on top of the potatoes, then the aubergines on top of the tomatoes. Beat the eggs with the yoghurt and Parmesan cheese and pour over the aubergine and tomatoes. Bake in the preheated oven for 25 minutes, or until golden and piping hot. Serve.

Try This: FOR AN ALTERNATIVE: 144 FOR A DIFFERENT MEAT OPTION: 66

Crown Roast of Lamb

SERVES 6

1 lamb crown roast
salt and freshly ground
    black pepper
1 tbsp sunflower oil
1 small onion, peeled and
    finely chopped
2–3 garlic cloves, peeled
    and crushed

2 celery stalks, trimmed
    and finely chopped
125 g/4 oz cooked mixed
    basmati and wild rice
75 g/3 oz ready-to-eat-dried
    apricots, chopped
50 g/2 oz pine nuts, toasted
1 tbsp finely grated

orange rind
2 tbsp freshly chopped
    coriander
1 small egg, beaten
freshly roasted potatoes and
    green vegetables, to serve

Preheat the oven to 180°C/350°F/Gas Mark 4, about 10 minutes before roasting. Wipe the crown roast and season the cavity with salt and pepper. Place in a roasting tin and cover the ends of the bones with small pieces of foil.

Heat the oil in a small saucepan and cook the onion, garlic and celery for 5 minutes, then remove the saucepan from the heat. Add the cooked rice with the apricots, pine nuts, orange rind and coriander. Season with salt and pepper, then stir in the egg and mix well.

Carefully spoon the prepared stuffing into the cavity of the lamb, then roast in the preheated oven for 1–1½ hours. Remove the lamb from the oven and remove and discard the foil from the bones. Return to the oven and continue to cook for a further 15 minutes, or until cooked to personal preference.

Remove from the oven and leave to rest for 10 minutes before serving with the roast potatoes and freshly cooked vegetables.

Try This: FOR AN ALTERNATIVE: 154 FOR A DIFFERENT MEAT OPTION: 92

Lamb Pilaf

SERVES 4

2 tbsp vegetable oil
25 g/1 oz flaked or
   slivered almonds
1 medium onion, peeled
   and finely chopped
1 medium carrot, peeled
   and finely chopped
1 celery stalk, trimmed
   and finely chopped
350 g/12 oz lean lamb,

   cut into chunks
¼ tsp ground cinnamon
¼ tsp chilli flakes
2 large tomatoes, skinned,
   deseeded and chopped
grated rind of 1 orange
350 g/12 oz easy-cook
   brown basmati rice
600 ml/1 pint vegetable
   or lamb stock

2 tbsp freshly snipped
   chives
3 tbsp freshly chopped
   coriander
salt and freshly ground
   black pepper

To garnish:
lemon slices
sprigs of fresh coriander

Preheat the oven to 140°C/275°F/Gas Mark 1. Heat the oil in a flameproof casserole with a tight-fitting lid and add the almonds. Cook for about 1 minute until just starting to brown, stirring often. Add the onion, carrot and celery and cook gently for a further 8–10 minutes until soft and lightly browned.

Increase the heat and add the lamb. Cook for a further 5 minutes until the lamb has changed colour. Add the ground cinnamon and chilli flakes and stir briefly before adding the tomatoes and orange rind.

Stir and add the rice, then the stock. Bring slowly to the boil and cover tightly. Transfer to the preheated oven and cook for 30–35 minutes until the rice is tender and the stock is absorbed.

Remove from the oven and leave to stand for 5 minutes before stirring in the chives and coriander. Season to taste with salt and pepper. Garnish with the lemon slices and sprigs of fresh coriander and serve immediately.

Try This: FOR AN ALTERNATIVE: 132   FOR A DIFFERENT MEAT OPTION: 70

Roast Leg of Lamb & Boulangère Potatoes

SERVES 6

1.1 kg/2½ lb potatoes, peeled
1 large onion, peeled
    and finely sliced
salt and freshly ground
    black pepper
2 tbsp olive oil

50 g/2 oz butter
200 ml/7 fl oz lamb stock
100 ml/3½ fl oz milk
2 kg/4½ lb leg of lamb
2–3 sprigs of fresh rosemary
6 large garlic cloves, peeled

    and finely sliced
6 anchovy fillets, drained
extra sprigs of fresh
    rosemary, to garnish

Preheat the oven to 230°C/450°F/Gas Mark 8. Finely slice the potatoes – a mandolin is the best tool for this. Layer the potatoes with the onion in a large roasting tin, seasoning each layer with salt and pepper. Drizzle about 1 tablespoon of the olive oil over the potatoes and add the butter in small pieces. Pour in the lamb stock and milk and reserve.

Make small incisions all over the lamb with the point of a small, sharp knife. Into each incision insert a small piece of rosemary, a sliver of garlic and a piece of anchovy fillet.

Drizzle the leg of lamb and its flavourings with the rest of the olive oil and season well. Place the meat directly on to a shelf in the preheated oven. Position the roasting tin of potatoes directly underneath to catch the juices during cooking. Roast for 15 minutes per 500 g/1 lb 2 oz (about 1 hour for a joint this size), reducing the oven temperature after 20 minutes to 200°C/400°F/Gas Mark 6.

When the lamb is cooked, remove from the oven and allow to rest for 10 minutes before carving. Meanwhile, increase the oven heat and cook the potatoes for a further 10–15 minutes to crisp up. Garnish with fresh rosemary sprigs and serve immediately with the lamb.

Try This: FOR AN ALTERNATIVE: 132 FOR A DIFFERENT MEAT OPTION: 244

Lancashire Hotpot

SERVES 4

1 kg/2¼ lb middle end neck of
    lamb, divided into cutlets
2 tbsp vegetable oil
2 large onions, peeled
    and sliced
2 tsp plain flour
150 ml/¼ pint vegetable

or lamb stock
700 g/1½ lb waxy potatoes,
    peeled and thickly sliced
salt and freshly ground
    black pepper
1 bay leaf
2 sprigs of fresh thyme

1 tbsp melted butter
2 tbsp freshly chopped
    herbs, to garnish
freshly cooked green beans,
    to serve

Preheat the oven to 170˚C/325˚F/Gas Mark 3. Trim any excess fat from the lamb cutlets. Heat the oil in a frying pan and brown the cutlets in batches for 3–4 minutes. Remove with a slotted spoon and reserve. Add the onions to the frying pan and cook for 6–8 minutes until softened and just beginning to colour, then remove and reserve.

Stir in the flour and cook for a few seconds, then gradually pour in the stock, stirring well, and bring to the boil. Remove from the heat.

Spread the base of a large casserole with half the potato slices. Top with half the onions and season well with salt and pepper. Arrange the browned meat in a layer. Season again and add the remaining onions, bay leaf and thyme. Pour in the remaining liquid from the onions and top with remaining potatoes so that they overlap in a single layer. Brush the potatoes with the melted butter and season again.

Cover the saucepan and cook in the preheated oven for 2 hours, uncovering for the last 30 minutes to allow the potatoes to brown. Garnish with chopped herbs and serve immediately with green beans.

 Try This: FOR AN ALTERNATIVE: 128 FOR A DIFFERENT MEAT OPTION: 264

Shepherd's Pie

SERVES 4

2 tbsp vegetable or olive oil
1 onion, peeled and finely chopped
1 carrot, peeled and finely chopped
1 celery stalk, trimmed and finely chopped
1 tbsp sprigs of fresh thyme

450 g/1 lb leftover roast lamb, finely chopped
150 ml/¼ pint red wine
150 ml/¼ pint lamb or vegetable stock or leftover gravy
2 tbsp tomato purée
salt and freshly ground

black pepper
700 g/1½ lb potatoes, peeled and cut into chunks
25 g/1 oz butter
6 tbsp milk
1 tbsp freshly chopped parsley
fresh herbs, to garnish

Preheat the oven to 200°C/400°F/Gas Mark 6, about 15 minutes before cooking. Heat the oil in a large saucepan and add the onion, carrot and celery. Cook over a medium heat for 8–10 minutes until softened and starting to brown.

Add the thyme and cook briefly, then add the cooked lamb, wine, stock and tomato purée. Season to taste with salt and pepper and simmer gently for 25–30 minutes until reduced and thickened. Remove from the heat to cool slightly and season again.

Meanwhile, boil the potatoes in plenty of salted water for 12–15 minutes until tender. Drain and return to the saucepan over a low heat to dry out. Remove from the heat and add the butter, milk and parsley. Mash until creamy, adding a little more milk if necessary. Adjust the seasoning.

Transfer the lamb mixture to a shallow ovenproof dish. Spoon the mash over the filling and spread evenly to cover completely. Fork the surface, place on a baking sheet, then cook in the preheated oven for 25–30 minutes until the potato topping is browned and the filling is piping hot. Garnish and serve.

 Try This: FOR AN ALTERNATIVE: 134   FOR A DIFFERENT MEAT OPTION: 62

Red Wine Risotto with Lambs' Kidneys & Caramelised Shallots

SERVES 4

8 lambs' kidneys, halved and cores removed
150 ml/¼ pint milk
2 tbsp olive oil
50 g/2 oz butter
275 g/10 oz shallots, peeled and halved if large

1 onion, peeled and finely chopped
2 garlic cloves, peeled and finely chopped
350 g/12 oz Arborio rice
225 ml/8 fl oz red wine
1 litre/1¾ pints chicken

or vegetable stock, heated
1 tbsp sprigs of fresh thyme
50 g/2 oz Parmesan cheese, grated
salt and freshly ground black pepper
fresh herbs, to garnish

Place the lambs' kidneys in a bowl and pour the milk over. Leave to soak for 15–20 minutes, then drain and pat dry on absorbent kitchen paper. Discard the milk.

Heat 1 tablespoon of the oil with 25 g/1 oz of the butter in a medium saucepan. Add the shallots, cover and cook for 10 minutes over a gentle heat. Remove the lid and cook for a further 10 minutes, or until tender and golden.

Meanwhile, heat the remaining oil with the remaining butter in a deep-sided frying pan. Add the onion and cook over a medium heat for 5–7 minutes until starting to brown. Add the garlic and cook briefly.

Stir in the rice and cook for a further minute until glossy and well coated in oil and butter. Add half the red wine and stir until absorbed. Add a ladleful or two of the stock and stir well until the stock is absorbed. Continue adding the stock, a ladleful at a time, and stirring well between additions, until all of the stock is added and the rice is just tender, but still firm. Remove from the heat.

Meanwhile, when the rice is nearly cooked, increase the heat under the shallots, add the thyme and kidneys. Cook for 3–4 minutes, then add the wine. Bring to the boil, then simmer rapidly until the red wine is reduced and syrupy. Stir the cheese into the rice with the caramelised shallots and kidneys. Season to taste, garnish and serve.

Try This: FOR AN ALTERNATIVE: 128   FOR A DIFFERENT MEAT OPTION: 68

Marinated Lamb Chops with Garlic Fried Potatoes

SERVES 4

4 thick lamb chump chops
3 tbsp olive oil
550 g/1¼ lb potatoes,
    peeled and cut into
    1 cm/½ inch dice
6 unpeeled garlic cloves
mixed salad or freshly cooked

vegetables, to serve

For the marinade:
1 small bunch of fresh
    thyme, leaves removed
1 tbsp freshly
    chopped rosemary

1 tsp salt
2 garlic cloves, peeled
    and crushed
rind and juice of 1 lemon
2 tbsp olive oil

Trim the chops of any excess fat, wipe with a clean damp cloth and reserve. To make the marinade, using a pestle and mortar, pound the thyme leaves and rosemary with the salt until pulpy. Add the garlic and continue pounding until crushed. Stir in the lemon rind and juice and the olive oil.

Pour the marinade over the lamb chops, turning them until they are well coated. Cover lightly and leave to marinate in the refrigerator for about 1 hour.

Meanwhile, heat the oil in a large non-stick frying pan. Add the potatoes and garlic and cook over a low heat for about 20 minutes, stirring occasionally. Increase the heat and cook for a further 10–15 minutes until golden. Drain on absorbent kitchen paper and add salt to taste. Keep warm.

Heat a griddle pan until almost smoking. Add the lamb chops and cook for 3–4 minutes on each side until golden, but still pink in the middle. Serve with the potatoes, and either a mixed salad or freshly cooked vegetables.

Try This: FOR AN ALTERNATIVE: 140   FOR A DIFFERENT MEAT OPTION: 98

Pappardelle with Spicy Lamb & Peppers

SERVES 4

450 g/1 lb fresh lamb mince
2 tbsp olive oil
1 onion, peeled and
    finely chopped
2 garlic cloves, peeled
    and crushed
1 green pepper, deseeded
    and chopped

1 yellow pepper, deseeded
    and chopped
½ tsp hot chilli powder
1 tsp ground cumin
1 tbsp tomato paste
150 ml/¼ pint red wine
salt and freshly ground
    black pepper

350 g/12 oz pappardelle
2 oz fresh white breadcrumbs
25 g/1 oz butter, melted
25 g/1 oz Cheddar
    cheese, grated
1 tbsp freshly chopped parsley

Preheat the grill just before cooking. Dry-fry the minced lamb in a frying pan until browned. Heat the olive oil in a heavy-based pan, add the onion, garlic and all the chopped peppers and cook gently for 3–4 minutes, or until softened. Add the browned lamb mince to the pan and cook stirring, until the onions have softened, then drain off any remaining oil.

Stir the chilli powder and cumin into the pan and cook gently for 2 minutes, stirring frequently. Add the tomato paste, pour in the wine and season to taste with salt and pepper. Reduce the heat and simmer for 10–15 minutes, or until the sauce has reduced.

Meanwhile, bring a large pan of lightly salted water to a rolling boil. Add the pappardelle and cook according to the packet instructions, or until 'al dente'. Drain thoroughly, then return to the pan and stir the meat sauce into the pasta. Keep warm.

Meanwhile, place the breadcrumbs on a baking tray, drizzle over the melted butter and place under the preheated grill for 3–4 minutes, or until golden and crispy. Allow to cool, then mix with the grated Cheddar cheese. Tip the pasta mixture into a warmed serving dish, sprinkle with the breadcrumbs and the parsley. Serve immediately.

Try This: FOR AN ALTERNATIVE: 158   FOR A DIFFERENT MEAT OPTION: 88

Lamb & Pasta Pie

SERVES 8

400 g/14 oz plain white flour
100 g/3½ oz margarine
100 g/3½ oz white
   vegetable fat
pinch of salt
1 small egg, separated
50 g/2 oz butter
50 g/2 oz flour

450 ml/¾ pint milk
salt and freshly ground
   black pepper
225 g/8 oz macaroni
50 g/2 oz Cheddar
   cheese, grated
1 tbsp vegetable oil
1 onion, peeled

and chopped
1 garlic clove, peeled
   and crushed
2 celery sticks, trimmed
   and chopped
450 g/1 lb lamb mince
1 tbsp tomato paste
400 g can chopped tomatoes

Preheat the oven to 190˚C/375˚F/Gas Mark 5, 10 minutes before cooking. Lightly oil a 20.5 cm/8 inch spring-form cake tin. Blend the flour, salt, margarine and white vegetable fat in a food processor and add sufficient cold water to make a smooth, pliable dough. Knead on a lightly floured surface, then roll out two thirds to line the base and sides of the tin. Brush the pastry with egg white and reserve.

Melt the butter in a heavy-based pan, stir in the flour and cook for 2 minutes. Stir in the milk and cook, stirring, until a smooth, thick sauce is formed. Season to taste with salt and pepper and reserve. Bring a large pan of lightly salted water to a rolling boil. Add the macaroni and cook according to the packet instructions, or until 'al dente'. Drain, then stir into the white sauce with the grated cheese.

Heat the oil in a frying pan, add the onion, garlic, celery and lamb mince and cook, stirring, for 5–6 minutes. Stir in the tomato paste and tomatoes and cook for 10 minutes. Cool slightly. Place half the pasta mixture, then all the mince in the pastry-lined tin. Top with a layer of pasta. Roll out the remaining pastry and cut out a lid. Brush the edge with water, place over the filling and pinch the edges together. Use trimmings to decorate the top of the pie. Brush the pie with beaten egg yolk and bake in the preheated oven for 50–60 minutes, covering the top with foil if browning too quickly. Stand for 15 minutes before turning out. Serve immediately.

Try This: FOR AN ALTERNATIVE: 160   FOR A DIFFERENT MEAT OPTION: 60

Roasted Lamb with Rosemary & Garlic

SERVES 6

1.6 kg/3½ lb leg of lamb
8 garlic cloves, peeled
few sprigs of fresh rosemary
salt and freshly ground
   black pepper

4 slices pancetta
4 tbsp olive oil
4 tbsp red wine vinegar
900 g/2 lb potatoes
1 large onion

sprigs of fresh rosemary,
   to garnish
freshly cooked ratatouille,
   to serve

Preheat oven to 200°C/400°F/Gas Mark 6, 15 minutes before roasting. Wipe the leg of lamb with a clean damp cloth, then place the lamb in a large roasting tin. With a sharp knife, make small, deep incisions into the meat. Cut 2–3 garlic cloves into small slivers, then insert with a few small sprigs of rosemary into the lamb. Season to taste with salt and pepper and cover the lamb with the slices of pancetta.

Drizzle over 1 tablespoon of the olive oil and lay a few more rosemary sprigs across the lamb. Roast in the preheated oven for 30 minutes, then pour over the vinegar.

Peel the potatoes and cut into large dice. Peel the onion and cut into thick wedges then thickly slice the remaining garlic. Arrange around the lamb. Pour the remaining olive oil over the potatoes, then reduce the oven temperature to 180°C/350°F/Gas Mark 4 and roast for a further 1 hour, or until the lamb is tender. Garnish with fresh sprigs of rosemary and serve immediately with the roast potatoes and ratatouille.

Try This: FOR AN ALTERNATIVE: 140 FOR A DIFFERENT MEAT OPTION: 244

Braised Lamb with Broad Beans

SERVES 4

700 g/1½ lb lamb, cut into
  large chunks
1 tbsp plain flour
1 onion
2 garlic cloves
1 tbsp olive oil

400 g can chopped tomatoes
  with basil
300 ml/½ pint lamb stock
2 tbsp freshly chopped thyme
2 tbsp freshly
  chopped oregano

salt and freshly ground
  black pepper
150 g/5 oz frozen broad beans
fresh oregano, to garnish
creamy mashed potatoes,
  to serve

Trim the lamb, discarding any fat or gristle, then place the flour in a polythene bag, add the lamb and toss until coated thoroughly. Peel and slice the onion and garlic and reserve. Heat the olive oil in a heavy-based saucepan and when hot, add the lamb and cook, stirring, until the meat is sealed and browned all over. Using a slotted spoon transfer the lamb to a plate and reserve.

Add the onion and garlic to the saucepan and cook for 3 minutes, stirring frequently until softened, then return the lamb to the saucepan. Add the chopped tomatoes with their juice, the stock, the chopped thyme and oregano to the pan and season to taste with salt and pepper. Bring to the boil, then cover with a close-fitting lid, reduce the heat and simmer for 1 hour.

Add the broad beans to the lamb and simmer for 20–30 minutes, or until the lamb is tender. Garnish with fresh oregano and serve with creamy mashed potatoes.

Try This: FOR AN ALTERNATIVE: 154   FOR A DIFFERENT MEAT OPTION: 74

Moroccan Penne

SERVES 4

1 tbsp sunflower oil
1 red onion, peeled
  and chopped
2 cloves garlic, peeled
  and crushed
1 tbsp coriander seeds
¼ tsp cumin seeds

¼ tsp freshly grated nutmeg
450 g/1 lb lean lamb mince
1 aubergine, trimmed
  and diced
400 g can chopped tomatoes
300 ml/½ pint vegetable stock
125 g/4 oz ready-to-eat

apricots, chopped
12 black olives, pitted
salt and freshly ground
  black pepper
350 g/12 oz penne
1 tbsp toasted pine nuts,
  to garnish

Preheat the oven to 200°C/400°F/Gas Mark 6, 15 minutes before using. Heat the sunflower oil in a large flameproof casserole. Add the chopped onion and fry for 5 minutes, or until softened.

Using a pestle and mortar, pound the garlic, coriander seeds, cumin seeds and grated nutmeg together into a paste. Add to the onion and cook for 3 minutes.

Add the lamb mince to the casserole and fry, stirring with a wooden spoon, for 4–5 minutes, or until the mince has broken up and browned.

Add the aubergine to the mince and fry for 5 minutes. Stir in the chopped tomatoes and vegetable stock and bring to the boil. Add the apricots and olives, then season well with salt and pepper. Return to the boil, lower the heat and simmer for 15 minutes.

Add the penne to the casserole, stir well, then cover and place in the preheated oven. Cook for 10 minutes then stir and return to the oven, uncovered, for a further 15–20 minutes, or until the pasta is 'al dente'. Remove from the oven, sprinkle with toasted pine nuts and serve immediately.

Try This: FOR AN ALTERNATIVE: 162 FOR A DIFFERENT MEAT OPTION: 280

Lamb Arrabbiata

SERVES 4

4 tbsp olive oil
450 g/1 lb lamb fillets, cubed
1 large onion, peeled
    and sliced
4 garlic cloves, peeled
    and finely chopped
1 red chilli, deseeded and

finely chopped
400 g can chopped tomatoes
175 g/6 oz pitted black
    olives, halved
150 ml/¼ pint white wine
salt and freshly ground
    black pepper

275 g/10 oz farfalle pasta
1 tsp butter
4 tbsp freshly chopped
    parsley, plus 1 tbsp
    to garnish

Heat 2 tablespoons of the olive oil in a large frying pan and cook the lamb for 5–7 minutes, or until sealed. Remove from the pan using a slotted spoon and reserve.

Heat the remaining oil in the pan, add the onion, garlic and chilli and cook until softened. Add the tomatoes, bring to the boil, then simmer for 10 minutes.

Return the browned lamb to the pan with the olives and pour in the wine. Bring the sauce back to the boil, reduce the heat then simmer, uncovered, for 15 minutes, or until the lamb is tender. Season to taste with salt and pepper.

Meanwhile, bring a large pan of lightly salted water to a rolling boil. Add the pasta and cook according to the packet instructions, or until 'al dente'.

Drain the pasta, toss in the butter, then add to the sauce and mix lightly. Stir in 4 tablespoons of the chopped parsley, then tip into a warmed serving dish. Sprinkle with the remaining parsley and serve immediately.

Try This: FOR AN ALTERNATIVE: 150   FOR A DIFFERENT MEAT OPTION: 90

Creamed Lamb & Wild Mushroom Pasta

SERVES 4

25 g/1 oz dried porcini
450 g/1 lb pasta shapes
25 g/1 oz butter
1 tbsp olive oil
350 g/12 oz lamb neck fillet, thinly sliced
1 garlic clove, peeled

and crushed
225 g/8 oz brown or wild mushrooms, wiped and sliced
4 tbsp white wine
125 ml/4 fl oz double cream
salt and freshly ground

black pepper
1 tbsp freshly chopped parsley, to garnish
freshly grated Parmesan cheese, to serve

Place the porcini in a small bowl and cover with almost boiling water. Leave to soak for 30 minutes. Drain the porcini, reserving the soaking liquid. Chop the porcini finely.

Bring a large pan of lightly salted water to a rolling boil. Add the pasta and cook according to the packet instructions, or until 'al dente'.

Meanwhile, melt the butter with the olive oil in a large frying pan and fry the lamb to seal. Add the garlic, mushrooms and prepared porcini and cook for 5 minutes, or until just soft.

Add the wine and the reserved porcini soaking liquid, then simmer for 2 minutes. Stir in the cream with the seasoning and simmer for 1–2 minutes, or until just thickened.

Drain the pasta thoroughly, reserving about 4 tablespoons of the cooking water. Return the pasta to the pan. Pour over the mushroom sauce and toss lightly together, adding the pasta water if the sauce is too thick. Tip into a warmed serving dish or spoon on to individual plates. Garnish with the chopped parsley and serve immediately with grated Parmesan cheese.

Try This: FOR AN ALTERNATIVE: 146   FOR A DIFFERENT MEAT OPTION: 74

Tagliatelle with Creamy Liver & Basil

SERVES 4

25 g/1 oz plain flour
salt and freshly ground
  black pepper
450 g/1 lb lamb's liver, thinly
  sliced and cut into
  bite-sized pieces
25 g/1 oz butter

1 tbsp olive oil
2 red onions, peeled
  and sliced
1 garlic clove, peeled
  and sliced
150 ml/¼ pint chicken stock
1 tbsp tomato paste

2 sun-dried tomatoes,
  finely chopped
1 tbsp freshly chopped basil
150 ml/¼ pint double cream
350 g/12 oz tagliatelle verdi
fresh basil leaves, to garnish

Season the flour lightly with salt and pepper and place in a large plastic bag. Add the liver and toss gently to coat. Remove the liver from the bag and reserve.

Melt the butter with the olive oil in a large frying pan. Add the onion and garlic and fry for 6–8 minutes, or until the onions begin to colour. Add the liver and fry until brown on all sides.

Stir in the chicken stock, tomato paste and sun-dried tomatoes. Bring to the boil, reduce the heat and simmer very gently for 10 minutes.

Meanwhile, bring a large pan of lightly salted water to a rolling boil. Add the pasta and cook according to the packet instructions, or until 'al dente'.

Stir the chopped basil and cream into the liver sauce and season to taste.

Drain the pasta thoroughly, reserving 2 tablespoons of the cooking water. Tip the pasta into a warmed serving dish or pile on to individual plates. Stir the reserved cooking water into the liver sauce and pour over the pasta. Toss lightly to coat the pasta. Garnish with basil leaves and serve immediately.

Try This: FOR AN ALTERNATIVE: 150   FOR A DIFFERENT MEAT OPTION: 252

Pork

Crispy Pork Wontons

SERVES 4

1 small onion, peeled
   and roughly chopped
2 garlic cloves, peeled
   and crushed
1 green chilli, deseeded
   and chopped
2.5 cm/1 inch piece fresh

root ginger, peeled
   and roughly chopped
450 g/1 lb lean pork mince
4 tbsp freshly chopped
   coriander
1 tsp Chinese five-
   spice powder

salt and freshly ground
   black pepper
20 wonton wrappers
1 medium egg,
   lightly beaten
vegetable oil for deep-frying
chilli sauce, to serve

Place the onion, garlic, chilli and ginger in a food processor and blend until very finely chopped. Add the pork, coriander and Chinese five-spice powder. Season to taste with salt and pepper, then blend again briefly to mix. Divide the mixture into 20 equal portions and with floured hands shape each into a walnut-sized ball.

Brush the edges of a wonton wrapper with beaten egg, place a pork ball in the centre, then bring the corners to the centre and pinch together to make a money bag. Repeat with the remaining pork balls and wrappers.

Pour sufficient oil into a heavy-based saucepan or deep-fat fryer so that it is one-third full and heat to 180°C/350°F. Deep-fry the wontons in 3 or 4 batches for 3–4 minutes, or until cooked through and golden and crisp. Drain on absorbent kitchen paper. Serve the crispy pork wontons immediately, allowing 5 per person, with some chilli sauce for dipping.

Try This: FOR AN ALTERNATIVE: 176 FOR A DIFFERENT MEAT OPTION: 24

Lion's Head Pork Balls

SERVES 4

75 g/3 oz glutinous rice
450 g/1 lb lean pork mince
2 garlic cloves, peeled
and crushed
1 tbsp cornflour
½ tsp Chinese five-
spice powder
2 tsp dark soy sauce

1 tbsp Chinese rice wine
or dry sherry
2 tbsp freshly
chopped coriander
salt and freshly ground
black pepper
**For the sweet chilli
dipping sauce:**

2 tsp caster sugar
1 tbsp sherry vinegar
1 tbsp light soy sauce
1 shallot, peeled and very
finely chopped
1 small red chilli, deseeded
and finely chopped
2 tsp sesame oil

Place the rice in a bowl and pour over plenty of cold water. Cover and soak for 2 hours. Tip into a sieve and drain well.

Place the pork, garlic, cornflour, Chinese five-spice powder, soy sauce, Chinese rice wine or sherry and coriander in a bowl. Season to taste with salt and pepper and mix together.

With slightly wet hands, shape the pork mixture into 20 walnut-sized balls, then roll in the rice to coat. Place the balls slightly apart in a steamer or a colander set over a saucepan of boiling water, cover and steam for 20 minutes, or until cooked through.

Meanwhile, make the dipping sauce. Stir together the sugar, vinegar and soy sauce until the sugar dissolves. Add the shallot, chilli and sesame oil and whisk together with a fork. Transfer to a small serving bowl, cover and leave to stand for at least 10 minutes before serving.

Remove the pork balls from the steamer and arrange them on a warmed serving platter. Serve immediately with the sweet chilli dipping sauce.

Try This: FOR AN ALTERNATIVE: 180   FOR A DIFFERENT MEAT OPTION: 116

Barbecue Pork Steamed Buns

SERVES 12

For the buns:
175–200 g/6–7 oz plain flour
1 tbsp dried yeast
125 ml/4 fl oz milk
2 tbsp sunflower oil
1 tbsp sugar
½ tsp salt
spring onion tassels,

to garnish
fresh green salad leaves,
    to serve

For the filling:
2 tbsp vegetable oil
1 small red pepper, deseeded
    and finely chopped

2 garlic cloves, peeled
    and finely chopped
225 g/8 oz cooked pork,
    finely chopped
50 g/2 oz light brown sugar
50 ml/2 fl oz tomato ketchup
1–2 tsp hot chilli powder,
    or to taste

Put 75 g/3 oz of the flour in a bowl and stir in the yeast. Heat the milk, oil, sugar and salt in a small saucepan until warm, stirring until the sugar has dissolved. Pour into the bowl and, with an electric mixer, beat on a low speed for 30 seconds, scraping down the sides of the bowl, until blended. Beat at high speed for 3 minutes, then with a wooden spoon, stir in as much of the remaining flour as possible, until a stiff dough forms. Shape into a ball, place in a lightly oiled bowl, cover with clingfilm and leave for 1 hour in a warm place, or until doubled in size.

To make the filling, heat a wok, add the oil and when hot, add the red pepper and garlic. Stir-fry for 4–5 minutes. Add the remaining ingredients and bring to the boil, stir-frying for 2–3 minutes until thick and syrupy. Cool and reserve. Punch down the dough and turn on to a lightly floured surface. Divide into 12 pieces and shape them into balls, then cover and leave to rest for 5 minutes. Roll each ball to a 7.5 cm/3 inch circle. Place a heaped tablespoon of filling in the centre of each. Dampen the edges, then bring them up and around the filling, pinching together to seal. Place seam-side down on a small square of non-stick baking parchment. Continue with the remaining dough and filling. Leave to rise for 10 minutes. Bring a large wok half-filled with water to the boil, place the buns in a lightly oiled Chinese steamer, without touching each other. Cover and steam for 20–25 minutes, then remove and cool slightly. Garnish with spring onion tassels and serve with salad leaves.

Try This: FOR AN ALTERNATIVE: 206   FOR A DIFFERENT MEAT OPTION: 50

Sticky Braised Spare Ribs

SERVES 4

900 g/2 lb meaty pork spare
ribs, cut crossways into
7.5 cm/3 inch pieces
125 ml/4 fl oz apricot nectar
or orange juice
50 ml/2 fl oz dry white wine
3 tbsp black bean sauce

3 tbsp tomato ketchup
2 tbsp clear honey
3–4 spring onions,
trimmed and chopped
2 garlic cloves, peeled
and crushed
grated zest of 1 small orange

salt and freshly ground
black pepper

To garnish:
spring onion tassels
lemon wedges

Put the spare ribs in the wok and add enough cold water to cover. Bring to the boil over a medium-high heat, skimming any scum that rises to the surface. Cover and simmer for 30 minutes, then drain and rinse the ribs.

Rinse and dry the wok and return the ribs to it. In a bowl, blend the apricot nectar or orange juice with the white wine, black bean sauce, tomato ketchup and the honey until smooth.

Stir in the spring onions, garlic cloves and grated orange zest. Stir well until mixed thoroughly.

Pour the mixture over the spare ribs in the wok and stir gently until the ribs are lightly coated. Place over a moderate heat and bring to the boil.

Cover then simmer, stirring occasionally, for 1 hour, or until the ribs are tender and the sauce is thickened and sticky. (If the sauce reduces too quickly or begins to stick, add water 1 tablespoon at a time until the ribs are tender.) Adjust the seasoning to taste, then transfer the ribs to a serving plate and garnish with spring onion tassels and lemon wedges. Serve immediately.

Try This: FOR AN ALTERNATIVE: 184   FOR A DIFFERENT MEAT OPTION: 130

Fried Pork–filled Wontons

MAKES 24

For the filling:
275 g/10 oz cooked pork, finely chopped
2–3 spring onions, trimmed and finely chopped
2.5 cm/1 inch piece fresh root ginger, grated
1 garlic clove, peeled and crushed
1 small egg, lightly beaten
1 tbsp soy sauce
1 tsp soft light brown sugar
1 tsp sweet chilli sauce or tomato ketchup
24–30 wonton wrappers, 8 cm/3½ inches square
300 ml/½ pint vegetable oil for deep frying

For the ginger dipping sauce:
4 tbsp soy sauce
1–2 tbsp rice or raspberry vinegar
2.5 cm/1 inch piece fresh root ginger, peeled and finely slivered
1 tbsp sesame oil
1 tbsp soft light brown sugar
2–3 dashes hot chilli sauce
spring onion tassels, to garnish

Place all the filling ingredients into a food processor and, using the pulse button, process until well blended. Do not overwork, the filling should have a coarse texture.

Lay out the wonton wrappers on a clean chopping board and put a teaspoon of the filling in the centre of each. Brush the edges with a little water and bring up 2 opposite corners of each square over the filling to form a triangle, pressing the edges firmly to seal. Dampen the 2 other corners and overlap them slightly, pressing firmly to seal, to form an oven-envelope shape, similar to a tortellini.

For the dipping sauce, stir together all the ingredients until the sugar is dissolved. Pour into a serving bowl and reserve.

Heat the oil in a large wok to 190°C/375°F, or until a small cube of bread browns in about 30 seconds. Working in batches of 5–6, fry until the wontons are crisp and golden, turning once or twice. Remove and drain on absorbent kitchen paper. Garnish with spring onion tassels and serve hot with the dipping sauce.

Try This: FOR AN ALTERNATIVE: 168   FOR A DIFFERENT MEAT OPTION: 116

Char Sui Pork & Noodle Salad

SERVES 4

200 g/7 oz flat rice noodles
4 tbsp black treacle
2 tbsp dark soy sauce
3 tbsp Chinese rice wine
   or dry sherry
3 star anise, roughly crushed
1 cinnamon stick
350 g/12 oz pork tenderloin,

in 1 piece
1 tbsp groundnut oil
2 garlic cloves, peeled
   and finely chopped
1 tsp freshly grated
   root ginger
3 spring onions, trimmed
   and sliced

125 g/4 oz pak choi,
   roughly chopped
2 tbsp light soy sauce
fresh coriander leaves,
   to garnish
prepared or bought plum
   sauce, to serve

Preheat the oven to 220°C/425°F/Gas Mark 7, 15 minutes before cooking. Soak the noodles in boiling water according to the packet directions. Drain and reserve. Place the treacle, soy sauce, Chinese rice wine or sherry, star anise and cinnamon into a small saucepan and stir over a gentle heat until mixed thoroughly, then reserve.

Trim the pork tenderloin of any excess fat and put into a shallow dish. Pour the cooled sauce over the tenderloin. Turn the pork, making sure it is completely coated in the sauce. Place in the refrigerator and leave to marinate for 4 hours, turning occasionally.

Remove the pork from its marinade and transfer to a roasting tin. Roast in the preheated oven for 12–14 minutes, basting once, until the pork is cooked through. Remove from the oven and leave until just warm.

Heat the wok, add the oil and when hot, add the garlic, ginger and spring onions. Stir-fry for 30 seconds before adding the pak choi. Stir-fry for a further 1 minute until the pak choi has wilted, then add the noodles and soy sauce. Toss for a few seconds until well mixed, then transfer to a large serving dish. Leave to cool. Thickly slice the pork fillet and add to the cooled noodles. Garnish with coriander leaves and serve with plum sauce.

Try This: FOR AN ALTERNATIVE: 174 FOR A DIFFERENT MEAT OPTION: 146

Dim Sum Pork Parcels

MAKES ABOUT 40

125 g/4 oz canned water
    chestnuts, drained and
    finely chopped
125 g/4 oz raw prawns,
    peeled, deveined and
    coarsely chopped
350 g/12 oz fresh pork mince
2 tbsp smoked bacon,
    finely chopped
1 tbsp light soy sauce, plus

    extra, to serve
1 tsp dark soy sauce
1 tbsp Chinese rice wine
2 tbsp fresh root ginger,
    peeled and finely chopped
3 spring onions, trimmed
    and finely chopped
2 tsp sesame oil
1 medium egg white,
    lightly beaten

salt and freshly ground
    black pepper
2 tsp sugar
40 wonton wrappers,
    thawed if frozen
toasted sesame seeds,
    to garnish
soy sauce, to serve

Place the water chestnuts, prawns, pork mince and bacon in a bowl and mix together. Add the soy sauces, Chinese rice wine, ginger, chopped spring onion, sesame oil and egg white. Season to taste with salt and pepper, sprinkle in the sugar and mix the filling thoroughly.

Place a spoonful of filling in the centre of a wonton wrapper. Bring the sides up and press around the filling to make a basket shape. Flatten the base of the wrapper, so the wonton stands solid. The top should be wide open, exposing the filling.

Place the parcels on a heatproof plate, on a wire rack inside a wok or on the base of a muslin-lined bamboo steamer. Place over a wok, half-filled with boiling water, cover, then steam the parcels for about 20 minutes. Do this in 2 batches. Transfer to a warmed serving plate, sprinkle with toasted sesame seeds, drizzle with soy sauce and serve immediately.

Try This: FOR AN ALTERNATIVE: 206   FOR A DIFFERENT MEAT OPTION: 30

Pork with Tofu

SERVES 4

450 g/1 lb smoked firm
  tofu, drained
2 tbsp groundnut oil
3 garlic cloves, peeled
  and crushed
2.5 cm/1 inch piece fresh
  root ginger, peeled and
finely chopped
350 g/12 oz fresh pork mince
1 tbsp chilli powder
1 tsp sugar
2 tbsp Chinese rice wine
1 tbsp dark soy sauce
1 tbsp light soy sauce
2 tbsp yellow bean sauce
1 tsp Szechuan peppercorns
75 ml/3 fl oz chicken stock
spring onions, trimmed and
  finely sliced, to garnish
fried rice, to serve

Cut the tofu into 1 cm/½ inch cubes and place in a sieve to drain. Place the tofu on absorbent kitchen paper to dry thoroughly for another 10 minutes.

Heat the wok, add the groundnut oil and when hot, add the garlic and ginger. Stir-fry for a few seconds to flavour the oil, but not to colour the vegetables. Add the pork mince and stir-fry for 3 minutes, or until the pork is sealed and there are no lumps in the mince.

Add all the remaining ingredients except for the tofu. Bring the mixture to the boil, then reduce the heat to low. Add the tofu and mix it in gently, taking care not to break up the tofu chunks, but ensuring an even mixture of ingredients. Simmer, uncovered, for 15 minutes, or until the tofu is tender. Turn into a warmed serving dish, garnish with sliced spring onions and serve immediately with fried rice.

Try This: FOR AN ALTERNATIVE: 194   FOR A DIFFERENT MEAT OPTION: 118

Apple–tossed Pork

SERVES 4

350 g/12 oz pork fillet
2 tbsp plain flour
salt and freshly ground
    black pepper
1½ tbsp sunflower oil

15 g/½ oz unsalted butter
2 dessert apples, peeled,
    cored and thinly sliced
2 tsp Dijon mustard
1 tbsp freshly chopped sage

2 tbsp Calvados brandy
4 tbsp crème fraîche
fresh sage leaves, to garnish
freshly cooked beans,
    to serve

Trim away any visible fat from the pork fillet, then cut across into 1 cm/½ inch thick slices. Season the flour, then add the pork slices a few at a time and toss until lightly coated.

Heat a wok, then add the oil and heat. Stir-fry the meat in 2 batches over a fairly high heat until well browned. Remove from the wok and reserve.

Melt the butter in the wok, add the apple slices and cook, stirring all the time, for 1 minute. Stir in the mustard, chopped sage, Calvados brandy and crème fraîche. Bring to the boil, stirring.

Return the pork and any juices to the wok and cook over a gentle heat for 1–2 minutes, or until the meat has warmed through, the apples are just tender and the sauce is bubbling. Spoon on to warmed plates, garnish with fresh sage leaves and serve immediately with freshly cooked green beans.

Try This: FOR AN ALTERNATIVE: 216   FOR A DIFFERENT MEAT OPTION: 122

Pork Fried Noodles

SERVES 4

125 g/4 oz dried thread
  egg noodles
125 g/4 oz broccoli florets
4 tbsp groundnut oil
350 g/12 oz pork tenderloin,
  cut into slices
3 tbsp soy sauce
1 tbsp lemon juice
pinch of sugar

1 tsp chilli sauce
1 tbsp sesame oil
2.5 cm/1 inch piece fresh
  root ginger, peeled
  and cut into sticks
1 garlic clove, peeled
  and chopped
1 green chilli, deseeded
  and sliced

125 g/4 oz mangetout, halved
  widthways
2 medium eggs, lightly beaten
227 g can water chestnuts,
  drained and sliced

To garnish:
radish rose
spring onion tassels

Place the noodles in a bowl and cover with boiling water. Leave to stand for 20 minutes, stirring occasionally, or until tender. Drain and reserve. Meanwhile, blanch the broccoli in a saucepan of lightly salted boiling water for 2 minutes. Drain, refresh under cold running water and reserve.

Heat a large wok or frying pan, add the groundnut oil and heat until just smoking. Add the pork and stir-fry for 5 minutes, or until browned. Using a slotted spoon, remove the pork slices and reserve.

Mix together the soy sauce, lemon juice, sugar, chilli sauce and sesame oil and reserve.

Add the ginger to the wok and stir-fry for 30 seconds. Add the garlic and chilli and stir-fry for 30 seconds. Add the reserved broccoli and stir-fry for 3 minutes. Stir in the mangetout, pork and reserved noodles with the beaten eggs and water chestnuts and stir-fry for 5 minutes or until heated through. Pour over the reserved chilli sauce, toss well and turn into a warmed serving dish. Garnish and serve immediately.

Try This: FOR AN ALTERNATIVE: 178   FOR A DIFFERENT MEAT OPTION: 306

Hoisin Pork

SERVES 4

1.4 kg/3 lb piece lean belly
   pork, boned
sea salt
2 tsp Chinese five-

spice powder
2 garlic cloves, peeled
   and chopped
1 tsp sesame oil

4 tbsp hoisin sauce
1 tbsp clear honey
assorted salad leaves,
   to garnish

Preheat the oven to 200°C/400°F/Gas Mark 6, 15 minutes before cooking. Using a sharp knife, cut the pork skin in a crisscross pattern, making sure not to cut all the way through into the flesh. Rub the salt evenly over the skin and leave to stand for 30 minutes.

Meanwhile, mix together the five-spice powder, garlic, sesame oil, hoisin sauce and honey until smooth. Rub the mixture evenly over the pork skin. Place the pork on a plate and chill in the refrigerator to marinate for up to 6 hours.

Place the pork on a wire rack set inside a roasting tin and roast the pork in the preheated oven for 1–1¼ hours, or until the pork is very crisp and the juices run clear when pierced with a skewer.

Remove the pork from the heat, leave to rest for 15 minutes, then cut into strips. Arrange on a warmed serving platter. Garnish with salad leaves and serve immediately.

Try This: FOR AN ALTERNATIVE: 218   FOR A DIFFERENT MEAT OPTION: 346

Pork Meatballs with Vegetables

SERVES 4

450 g/1 lb pork mince
2 tbsp freshly
   chopped coriander
2 garlic cloves, peeled
   and chopped
1 tbsp light soy sauce
salt and freshly ground
   black pepper
2 tbsp groundnut oil

2.5 cm/1 inch piece fresh
   root ginger, peeled and
   cut into matchsticks
1 red pepper, deseeded
   and cut into chunks
1 green pepper, deseeded
   and cut into chunks
2 courgettes, trimmed
   and cut into sticks

125 g/4 oz baby sweetcorn,
   halved lengthways
3 tbsp light soy sauce
1 tsp sesame oil
fresh coriander leaves,
   to garnish
freshly cooked noodles,
   to serve

Mix together the pork mince, the chopped coriander, half the garlic and the soy sauce, then season to taste with salt and pepper. Divide into 20 portions and roll into balls. Place on a baking sheet, cover with clingfilm and chill in the refrigerator for at least 30 minutes.

Heat a wok or large frying pan, add the groundnut oil and when hot, add the meatballs and cook for 8–10 minutes, or until the pork balls are browned all over, turning occasionally. Using a slotted spoon, transfer the balls to a plate and keep warm.

Add the ginger and remaining garlic to the wok and stir-fry for 30 seconds. Add the red and green peppers and stir-fry for 5 minutes. Add the courgettes and sweetcorn and stir-fry for 3 minutes.

Return the pork balls to the wok, add the soy sauce and sesame oil and stir-fry for 1 minute, until heated through. Garnish with coriander leaves and serve immediately on a bed of noodles.

Try This: FOR AN ALTERNATIVE: 222   FOR A DIFFERENT MEAT OPTION: 114

Spicy Pork

SERVES 4

4 tbsp groundnut oil
2.5 cm/1 inch piece fresh
   root ginger, peeled and
   cut into matchsticks
1 garlic clove, peeled
   and chopped
2 medium carrots, peeled
   and cut into matchsticks

1 medium aubergine,
   trimmed and cubed
700 g/1½ lb pork fillet,
   thickly sliced
400 ml/14 fl oz coconut milk
2 tbsp Thai red curry paste
4 tbsp Thai fish sauce
2 tsp caster sugar

227 g can bamboo shoots in
   brine, drained and cut
   into matchsticks
salt, to taste
lime zest, to garnish
freshly cooked rice, to serve

Heat a wok or large frying pan, add 2 tablespoons of the oil and when hot, add the ginger, garlic, carrots and aubergine and stir-fry for 3 minutes. Using a slotted spoon, transfer to a plate and keep warm.

Add the remaining oil to the wok, heat until smoking, then add the pork and stir-fry for 5–8 minutes or until browned all over. Transfer to a plate and keep warm. Wipe the wok clean.

Pour half the coconut milk into the wok, stir in the red curry paste and bring to the boil. Boil rapidly for 4 minutes, stirring occasionally, or until the sauce is reduced by half.

Add the fish sauce and sugar to the wok and bring back to the boil. Return the pork and vegetables to the wok with the bamboo shoots. Return to the boil, then simmer for 4 minutes.

Stir in the remaining coconut milk and season to taste with salt. Simmer for 2 minutes or until heated through. Garnish with lime zest and serve immediately with rice.

Try This: FOR AN ALTERNATIVE: 194 FOR A DIFFERENT MEAT OPTION: 118

Pork with Tofu & Coconut

SERVES 4

50 g/2 oz unsalted cashew nuts
1 tbsp ground coriander
1 tbsp ground cumin
2 tsp hot chilli powder
2.5 cm/1 inch piece fresh root ginger, peeled and chopped
1 tbsp oyster sauce
4 tbsp groundnut oil

400 ml/14 fl oz coconut milk
175 g/6 oz rice noodles
450 g/1 lb pork tenderloin, thickly sliced
1 red chilli, deseeded and sliced
1 green chilli, deseeded and sliced
1 bunch spring onions,

trimmed and thickly sliced
3 tomatoes, roughly chopped
75 g/3 oz tofu, drained
2 tbsp freshly chopped coriander
2 tbsp freshly chopped mint
salt and freshly ground black pepper

Place the cashew nuts, coriander, cumin, chilli powder, ginger and oyster sauce in a food processor and blend until well ground. Heat a wok or large frying pan, add 2 tablespoons of the oil and when hot, add the cashew mixture and stir-fry for 1 minute. Stir in the coconut milk, bring to the boil, then simmer for 1 minute. Pour into a small jug and reserve. Wipe the wok clean.

Meanwhile, place the rice noodles in a bowl, cover with boiling water, leave to stand for 5 minutes, then drain thoroughly.

Reheat the wok, add the remaining oil and when hot, add the pork and stir-fry for 5 minutes or until browned all over. Add the chillies and spring onions and stir-fry for 2 minutes.

Add the tomatoes and tofu to the wok with the noodles and coconut mixture and stir-fry for a further 2 minutes, or until heated through, being careful not to break up the tofu. Sprinkle with the chopped coriander and mint, season to taste with salt and pepper and stir. Tip into a warmed serving dish and serve immediately.

 Try This: FOR AN ALTERNATIVE: 182   FOR A DIFFERENT MEAT OPTION: 308

Pork with Black Bean Sauce

SERVES 4

700 g/1½ lb pork tenderloin
4 tbsp light soy sauce
2 tbsp groundnut oil
1 garlic clove, peeled
   and chopped
2.5 cm/1 inch piece fresh
   root ginger, peeled and

cut into matchsticks
1 large carrot, peeled
   and sliced
1 red pepper, deseeded
   and sliced
1 green pepper, deseeded
   and sliced

160 g jar black bean sauce
salt
snipped fresh chives,
   to garnish
freshly steamed rice, to serve

Using a sharp knife, trim the pork, discarding any fat or sinew and cut into bite-sized chunks. Place in a large shallow dish and spoon over the soy sauce. Turn to coat evenly, cover with clingfilm and leave to marinate in the refrigerator for at least 30 minutes. When ready to use, lift the pork from the marinade, shaking off as much marinade as possible, and pat dry with absorbent kitchen paper. Reserve the marinade.

Heat a wok, add the groundnut oil and when hot, add the chopped garlic and ginger and stir-fry for 30 seconds. Add the carrot and the red and green peppers and stir-fry for 3–4 minutes or until just softened.

Add the pork to the wok and stir-fry for 5–7 minutes, or until browned all over and tender. Pour in the reserved marinade and black bean sauce. Bring to the boil, stirring constantly until well blended, then simmer for 1 minute, until heated through thoroughly. Tip into a warmed serving dish or spoon on to individual plates. Garnish with snipped chives and serve immediately with steamed rice.

Try This: FOR AN ALTERNATIVE: 218   FOR A DIFFERENT MEAT OPTION: 304

Pork Spring Rolls

SERVES 4

125 g/4 oz pork tenderloin
2 tbsp light soy sauce
225 ml/8 fl oz groundnut oil
1 medium carrot, peeled and
  cut into matchsticks
75 g/3 oz button
  mushrooms, wiped

and sliced
4 spring onions, trimmed
  and thinly sliced
75 g/3 oz beansprouts
1 garlic clove, peeled
  and chopped
1 tbsp dark soy sauce

12 large sheets filo pastry
  folded in half
spring onion curls,
  to garnish
Chinese-style dipping sauce,
  to serve

Trim the pork, discarding any sinew or fat, and cut into very fine strips. Place in a small bowl, pour over the light soy sauce and stir until well coated. Cover with clingfilm and leave to marinate in the refrigerator for at least 30 minutes.

Heat a wok or large frying pan, add 1 tablespoon of the oil and when hot, add the carrot and mushrooms and stir-fry for 3 minutes or until softened. Add the spring onions, beansprouts and garlic, stir-fry for 2 minutes, then transfer the vegetables to a bowl and reserve.

Drain the pork well, add to the wok and stir-fry for 2–4 minutes or until browned. Add the pork to the vegetables and leave to cool. Stir in the dark soy sauce and mix the filling well.

Lay the folded filo pastry sheets on a work surface. Divide the filling between the sheets, placing it at one end. Brush the filo edges with water, then fold the sides over and roll up.

Heat the remaining oil in a large wok to 180°C/350°F and cook the spring rolls in batches for 2–3 minutes, or until golden, turning the rolls during cooking. Using a slotted spoon, remove and drain on absorbent kitchen paper. Garnish with spring onion curls and serve immediately with a Chinese-style dipping sauce.

Try This: FOR AN ALTERNATIVE: 208   FOR A DIFFERENT MEAT OPTION: 292

Special Fried Rice

SERVES 4

25 g/1 oz butter
4 medium eggs, beaten
4 tbsp vegetable oil
1 bunch spring onions,
   trimmed and shredded
225 g/8 oz cooked ham, diced
125 g/4 oz large cooked

prawns with tails left on
75 g/3 oz peas, thawed
   if frozen
200 g can water chestnuts,
   drained and
   roughly chopped
450 g/1 lb cooked long-

grain rice
3 tbsp dark soy sauce
1 tbsp dry sherry
2 tbsp freshly chopped
   coriander
salt and freshly ground
   black pepper

Melt the butter in a wok or large frying pan and pour in half the beaten egg. Cook for 4 minutes drawing the edges of the omelette in to allow the uncooked egg to set into a round shape. Using a fish slice, lift the omelette from the wok and roll into a sausage shape. Leave to cool completely then using a sharp knife slice the omelette into rings.

Wipe the wok with absorbent kitchen paper and return to the heat. Add the oil and when hot, add the spring onions, ham, prawns, peas and chopped water chestnuts and stir-fry for 2 minutes. Add the rice and stir-fry for a further 3 minutes.

Add the remaining beaten eggs and stir-fry for 3 minutes, or until the egg has scrambled and set. Stir in the soy sauce, sherry and chopped coriander. Season to taste with salt and pepper and heat through thoroughly. Add the omelette rings and stir gently without breaking up the egg too much. Serve immediately.

Try This: FOR AN ALTERNATIVE: 250   FOR A DIFFERENT MEAT OPTION: 56

Cashew & Pork Stir Fry

SERVES 4

450 g/1 lb pork tenderloin
4 tbsp soy sauce
1 tbsp cornflour
125 g/4 oz unsalted
cashew nuts
4 tbsp sunflower oil
450 g/1 lb leeks, trimmed

and shredded
2.5 cm/1 inch piece fresh
root ginger, peeled and
cut into matchsticks
2 garlic cloves, peeled
and chopped
1 red pepper, deseeded

and sliced
300 ml/½ pint chicken stock
2 tbsp freshly chopped
coriander
freshly cooked noodles,
to serve

Using a sharp knife, trim the pork, discarding any sinew or fat. Cut into 2 cm/¾ inch slices and place in a shallow dish. Blend the soy sauce and cornflour together until smooth and free from lumps, then pour over the pork. Stir until coated in the cornflour mixture, then cover with clingfilm and leave to marinate in the refrigerator for at least 30 minutes.

Heat a nonstick frying pan until hot, add the cashew nuts and dry-fry for 2–3 minutes, or until toasted, stirring frequently. Transfer to a plate and reserve.

Heat a wok or large frying pan, add 2 tablespoons of the oil and when hot, add the leeks, ginger, garlic and pepper and stir-fry for 5 minutes or until softened. Using a slotted spoon, transfer to a plate and keep warm.

Drain the pork, reserving the marinade. Add the remaining oil to the wok and when hot, add the pork and stir-fry for 5 minutes or until browned. Return the reserved vegetables to the wok with the marinade and the stock. Bring to the boil, then simmer for 2 minutes, or until the sauce has thickened. Stir in the toasted cashew nuts and chopped coriander and serve immediately with freshly cooked noodles.

Try This: FOR AN ALTERNATIVE: 216   FOR A DIFFERENT MEAT OPTION: 312

Barbecue Pork Fillet

SERVES 4

2 tbsp clear honey
2 tbsp hoisin sauce
2 tsp tomato purée
2.5 cm/1 inch piece fresh
   root ginger, peeled
   and chopped
450 g/1 lb pork tenderloin
3 tbsp vegetable oil

1 garlic clove, peeled
   and chopped
1 bunch spring onions,
   trimmed and chopped
1 red pepper, deseeded and
   cut into chunks
1 yellow pepper, deseeded
   and cut into chunks

350 g/12 oz cooked
   long-grain rice
125 g/4 oz frozen peas,
   thawed
2 tbsp light soy sauce
1 tbsp sesame oil
50 g/2 oz toasted
   flaked almonds

Preheat the oven to 200°C/400°F/Gas Mark 6, 15 minutes before cooking. Mix together the honey, hoisin sauce, tomato purée and ginger in a bowl. Trim the pork, discarding any sinew or fat. Place in a shallow dish and spread the honey and hoisin sauce over the pork to cover completely. Cover with clingfilm and chill in the refrigerator for 4 hours, turning occasionally.

Remove the pork from the marinade and place in a roasting tin, reserving the marinade. Cook in the preheated oven for 20–25 minutes, or until the pork is tender and the juices run clear when pierced with a skewer. Baste occasionally during cooking with the reserved marinade. Remove the pork from the oven, leave to rest for 5 minutes, then slice thinly and keep warm.

Meanwhile, heat a wok or large frying pan, add the vegetable oil and when hot, add the garlic, spring onions and peppers and stir-fry for 4 minutes or until softened. Add the rice and peas and stir-fry for 2 minutes.

Add the soy sauce, sesame oil and flaked almonds and stir-fry for 30 seconds or until heated through. Tip into a warmed serving dish and top with the sliced pork. Serve immediately.

Try This: FOR AN ALTERNATIVE: 172 FOR A DIFFERENT MEAT OPTION: 66

Pork Cabbage Parcels

SERVES 4

8 large green cabbage leaves
1 tbsp vegetable oil
2 celery stalks, trimmed
    and chopped
1 carrot, peeled and cut
    into matchsticks
125 g/4 oz fresh pork mince
50 g/2 oz button mushrooms,
    wiped and sliced

1 tsp Chinese five-
    spice powder
50 g/2 oz cooked
    long-grain rice
juice of 1 lemon
1 tbsp soy sauce
150 ml/¼ pint chicken stock

For the tomato sauce:
1 tbsp vegetable oil
1 bunch spring onions,
    trimmed and chopped
400 g can chopped tomatoes
1 tbsp light soy sauce
1 tbsp freshly chopped mint
freshly ground black pepper

Preheat the oven to 180°C/350°F/Gas Mark 4, 10 minutes before cooking. To make the sauce, heat the oil in a heavy-based saucepan, add the spring onions and cook for 2 minutes or until softened.

Add the tomatoes, soy sauce and mint to the saucepan, bring to the boil, cover, then simmer for 10 minutes. Season to taste with pepper. Reheat when required.

Meanwhile, blanch the cabbage leaves in a large saucepan of lightly salted water for 3 minutes. Drain and refresh under cold running water. Pat dry with absorbent kitchen paper and reserve.

Heat the oil in a small saucepan, add the celery, carrot and pork mince and cook for 3 minutes. Add the mushrooms and cook for 3 minutes. Stir in the Chinese five-spice powder, rice, lemon juice and soy sauce and heat through.

Place some of the filling in the centre of each cabbage leaf and fold to enclose the filling. Place in a shallow ovenproof dish seam-side down. Pour over the stock and cook in the preheated oven for 30 minutes. Serve immediately with the reheated tomato sauce.

Try This: FOR AN ALTERNATIVE: 172   FOR A DIFFERENT MEAT OPTION: 30

Crispy Pork with Tangy Sauce

SERVES 4

350 g/12 oz pork fillet
1 tbsp light soy sauce
1 tbsp dry sherry
salt and freshly ground
    black pepper
1 tbsp sherry vinegar
1 tbsp tomato paste

1 tbsp dark soy sauce
2 tsp light muscovado sugar
150 ml/¼ pint chicken stock
1½ tsp clear honey
8 tsp cornflour
450 ml/¾ pint groundnut
    oil for frying

1 medium egg

To garnish:
fresh sprigs of dill
orange wedges

Remove and discard any fat and sinew from the pork fillet, then cut into 2 cm/¾ inch cubes and place in a shallow dish. Blend the light soy sauce with the dry sherry and add seasoning. Pour over the pork and stir until the pork is lightly coated. Cover and leave to marinate in the refrigerator for at least 30 minutes, stirring occasionally.

Meanwhile, blend the sherry vinegar, tomato paste, dark soy sauce, light muscovado sugar, chicken stock and honey together in a small saucepan and heat gently, stirring occasionally, until the sugar has dissolved. Then bring to the boil.

Blend 2 teaspoons of cornflour with 1 tablespoon of water and stir into the sauce. Cook, stirring, until smooth and thickened, and either keep warm or reheat when required.

Heat the oil in the wok to 190°C/375°F. Whisk together the remaining 6 teaspoons of cornflour and the egg to make a smooth batter. Drain the pork if necessary, then dip the pieces into the batter, allowing any excess to drip back into the bowl. Cook in the hot oil for 2–3 minutes, or until golden and tender. Drain on kitchen paper. Cook the pork in batches until it is all cooked, then garnish and serve immediately with the sauce.

Try This: FOR AN ALTERNATIVE: 168 FOR A DIFFERENT MEAT OPTION: 300

Caribbean Pork

SERVES 4

450 g/1 lb pork fillet
2.5 cm/1 inch piece fresh
   root ginger, peeled
   and grated
½ tsp crushed dried chillies
2 garlic cloves, peeled
   and crushed

2 tbsp freshly chopped parsley
150 ml/¼ pint orange juice
2 tbsp dark soy sauce
2 tbsp groundnut oil
1 large onion, peeled and
   sliced into wedges
1 large courgette (about

225 g/8 oz), trimmed and
   cut into strips
1 orange pepper, deseeded
   and cut into strips
1 ripe but firm mango,
   peeled and pitted
freshly cooked rice to serve

Cut the pork fillet into thin strips and place in a shallow dish. Sprinkle with the ginger, chillies, garlic and 1 tablespoon of the parsley. Blend together the orange juice, soy sauce and 1 tablespoon of the oil, then pour over the pork. Cover and chill in the refrigerator for 30 minutes, stirring occasionally. Remove the pork strips with a slotted spoon and reserve the marinade.

Heat the wok, pour in the remaining oil and stir-fry the pork for 3–4 minutes. Add the onion rings and the courgette and pepper strips and cook for 2 minutes. Add the reserved marinade to the wok and stir-fry for a further 2 minutes.

Cut the mango flesh into strips, then stir it into the pork mixture. Continue to stir-fry until everything is piping hot. Garnish with the remaining parsley and serve immediately with plenty of freshly cooked rice.

Try This: FOR AN ALTERNATIVE: 232 FOR A DIFFERENT MEAT OPTION: 344

Sausage & Bacon Risotto

SERVES 4

225 g/8 oz long-grain rice
1 tbsp olive oil
25 g/1 oz butter
175 g/6 oz cocktail sausages
1 shallot, peeled and
    finely chopped
75 g/3 oz bacon lardons or

thick slices of streaky
    bacon, chopped
150 g/5 oz chorizo or similar
    spicy sausage, cut
    into chunks
1 green pepper, deseeded
    and cut into strips

197 g can sweetcorn,
    drained
2 tbsp freshly chopped
    parsley
50 g/2 oz mozzarella
    cheese, grated

Cook the rice in a saucepan of boiling salted water for 15 minutes or until tender, or according to packet instructions. Drain and rinse in cold water. Drain again and leave until completely cold.

Meanwhile, heat the wok, pour in the oil and melt the butter. Cook the cocktail sausages, turning continuously until cooked. Remove with a slotted spoon, cut in half and keep warm.

Add the chopped shallot and bacon to the wok and cook for 2–3 minutes until cooked but not browned. Add the spicy sausage and green pepper and stir-fry for a further 3 minutes.

Add the cold rice and the sweetcorn to the wok and stir-fry for 2 minutes, then return the cooked sausages to the wok and stir over the heat until everything is piping hot. Garnish with the freshly chopped parsley and serve immediately with a little grated mozzarella cheese.

Try This: FOR AN ALTERNATIVE: 240   FOR A DIFFERENT MEAT OPTION: 326

Speedy Pork with Yellow Bean Sauce

SERVES 4

450 g/1 lb pork fillet
2 tbsp light soy sauce
2 tbsp orange juice
2 tsp cornflour
3 tbsp groundnut oil
2 garlic cloves, peeled

and crushed
175 g/6 oz carrots, peeled
and cut into matchsticks
125 g/4 oz fine green beans,
trimmed and halved
2 spring onions, trimmed

and cut into strips
4 tbsp yellow bean sauce
1 tbsp freshly chopped flat-
leaf parsley, to garnish
freshly cooked egg noodles,
to serve

Remove any fat or sinew from the pork fillet, and cut into thin strips. Blend the soy sauce, orange juice and cornflour in a bowl and mix thoroughly. Place the meat in a shallow dish, pour over the soy sauce mixture, cover and leave to marinate in the refrigerator for 1 hour. Drain with a slotted spoon, reserving the marinade.

Heat the wok, then add 2 tablespoons of the oil and stir-fry the pork with the garlic for 2 minutes, or until the meat is sealed. Remove with a slotted spoon and reserve.

Add the remaining oil to the wok and cook the carrots, beans and spring onions for about 3 minutes, until tender but still crisp. Return the pork to the wok with the reserved marinade, then pour over the yellow bean sauce. Stir-fry for a further 1–2 minutes, or until the pork is tender. Sprinkle with the chopped parsley and serve immediately with freshly cooked egg noodles.

Try This: FOR AN ALTERNATIVE: 196   FOR A DIFFERENT MEAT OPTION: 304

Honey Pork with Rice Noodles & Cashews

SERVES 4

125 g/4 oz rice noodles
450 g/1 lb pork fillet
2 tbsp groundnut oil
1 tbsp softened butter
1 onion, peeled and finely sliced into rings
2 garlic cloves, peeled

and crushed
125 g/4 oz baby button mushrooms, halved
3 tbsp light soy sauce
3 tbsp clear honey
50 g/2 oz unsalted cashew nuts

1 red chilli, deseeded and finely chopped
4 spring onions, trimmed and finely chopped
freshly stir-fried vegetables, to serve

Soak the rice noodles in boiling water for 4 minutes or according to packet instructions, then drain and reserve.

Trim and slice the pork fillet into thin strips. Heat the wok, pour in the oil and butter, and stir-fry the pork for 4–5 minutes, until cooked. Remove with a slotted spoon and keep warm.

Add the onion to the wok and stir-fry gently for 2 minutes. Stir in the garlic and mushrooms and cook for a further 2 minutes, or until juices start to run from the mushrooms.

Blend the soy sauce with the honey then return the pork to the wok with this mixture. Add the cashew nuts and cook for 1–2 minutes, then add the rice noodles a little at a time. Stir-fry until everything is piping hot. Sprinkle with chopped chilli and spring onions. Serve immediately with freshly stir-fried vegetables.

Try This: FOR AN ALTERNATIVE: 202   FOR A DIFFERENT MEAT OPTION: 312

Sweet-&-Sour Pork

SERVES 4

450 g/1 lb pork fillet
1 medium egg white
4 tsp cornflour
salt and freshly ground
  black pepper
300 ml/½ pint groundnut oil
1 small onion, peeled and
  finely sliced

125 g/4 oz carrots, peeled
  and cut into matchsticks
2.5 cm/1 inch piece fresh
  root ginger, peeled and
  cut into thin strips
150 ml/¼ pint orange juice
150 ml/¼ pint chicken stock
1 tbsp light soy sauce

220 g can pineapple
  pieces, drained and
  juice reserved
1 tbsp white wine vinegar
1 tbsp freshly
  chopped parsley
freshly cooked rice, to serve

Trim the pork fillet, then cut into small cubes. In a bowl, whisk the egg white and cornflour with a little seasoning, then add the pork to the egg white mixture and stir until the cubes are well coated.

Heat the wok, then add the oil and heat until very hot before adding the pork and stir-frying for 30 seconds. Turn off the heat and continue to stir for 3 minutes. The meat should be white and sealed. Drain off the oil, reserve the pork and wipe the wok clean.

Pour 2 teaspoons of the drained groundnut oil back into the wok and cook the onion, carrots and ginger for 2–3 minutes. Blend the orange juice with the chicken stock and soy sauce and make up to 300 ml/½ pint with the reserved pineapple juice.

Return the pork to the wok with the juice mixture and simmer for 3–4 minutes. Then stir in the pineapple pieces and vinegar. Heat through, then sprinkle with the chopped parsley and serve immediately with freshly cooked rice.

Try This: FOR AN ALTERNATIVE: 184   FOR A DIFFERENT MEAT OPTION: 322

Pork in Peanut Sauce

SERVES 4

450 g/1 lb pork fillet
2 tbsp light soy sauce
1 tbsp vinegar
1 tsp sugar
1 tsp Chinese five-spice
  powder
2–4 garlic cloves, peeled
  and crushed
2 tbsp groundnut oil

1 large onion, peeled and
  finely sliced
125 g/4 oz carrots, peeled
  and cut into matchsticks
2 celery sticks, trimmed
  and sliced
125 g/4 oz French beans,
  trimmed and halved
3 tbsp smooth peanut butter

1 tbsp freshly chopped flat-
  leaf parsley

To serve:
freshly cooked basmati and
  wild rice
green salad

Remove any fat or sinew from the pork fillet, cut into thin strips and reserve. Blend the soy sauce, vinegar, sugar, Chinese five-spice powder and garlic in a bowl and add the pork. Cover and leave to marinate in the refrigerator for at least 30 minutes.

Drain the pork, reserving any marinade. Heat the wok, then add the oil and when hot, stir-fry the pork for 3–4 minutes, or until sealed.

Add the onion, carrots, celery and beans to the wok and stir-fry for 4–5 minutes, or until the meat is tender and the vegetables are softened.

Blend the reserved marinade, the peanut butter and 2 tablespoons of hot water together. When smooth, stir into the wok and cook for several minutes more until the sauce is thick and the pork is piping hot. Sprinkle with the chopped parsley and serve immediately with the basmati and wild rice and a green salad.

Try This: FOR AN ALTERNATIVE: 216   FOR A DIFFERENT MEAT OPTION: 318

Pork with Spring Vegetables & Sweet Chilli Sauce

SERVES 4

450 g/1 lb pork fillet
2 tbsp sunflower oil
2 garlic cloves, peeled
  and crushed
2.5 cm/1 inch piece fresh root
  ginger, peeled and grated

125 g/4 oz carrots, peeled
  and cut into matchsticks
4 spring onions, trimmed
125 g/4 oz sugar snap peas
125 g/4 oz baby sweetcorn
2 tbsp sweet chilli sauce

2 tbsp light soy sauce
1 tbsp vinegar
½ tsp sugar, or to taste
125 g/4 oz beansprouts
grated zest of 1 orange
freshly cooked rice, to serve

Trim the pork fillet, then cut into thin strips and reserve. Heat a wok and pour in the oil. When hot, add the garlic and ginger and stir-fry for 30 seconds. Add the carrots to the wok and continue to stir-fry for 1–2 minutes, or until they start to soften.

Slice the spring onions lengthways, then cut into 3 lengths. Trim the sugar snap peas and the sweetcorn. Add the spring onions, sugar snap peas and sweetcorn to the wok and stir-fry for 30 seconds.

Add the pork to the wok and continue to stir-fry for 2–3 minutes, or until the meat is sealed and browned all over. Blend the sweet chilli sauce, soy sauce, vinegar and sugar together, then stir into the wok with the beansprouts.

Continue to stir-fry until the meat is cooked and the vegetables are tender but still crisp. Sprinkle with the orange zest and serve immediately with the freshly cooked rice.

Try This: FOR AN ALTERNATIVE: 190 FOR A DIFFERENT MEAT OPTION: 300

Pork with Assorted Peppers

SERVES 4

450 g/1 lb pork fillet
2 tbsp groundnut oil
1 onion, peeled and
    thinly sliced
1 red pepper, deseeded
    and cut into strips
1 yellow pepper, deseeded
    and cut into strips

1 orange pepper, deseeded
    and cut into strips
2 garlic cloves, peeled
    and crushed
2 tsp paprika
400 g can chopped tomatoes
300 ml/½ pint pork or
    chicken stock

1 tsp soft dark brown sugar
salt and freshly ground
    black pepper
handful fresh oregano leaves
350 g/12 oz penne
2 tbsp grated
    mozzarella cheese

Trim the pork fillet, discarding any sinew and fat, then cut into small cubes. Heat the wok, add the oil and when hot, stir-fry the pork for 3–4 minutes until they are brown and sealed. Remove the pork from the wok and reserve.

Add the sliced onions to the wok and stir-fry until they are softened, but not browned, then add the pepper strips and stir-fry for a further 3–4 minutes.

Stir in the garlic, paprika, chopped tomatoes, stock, sugar and seasoning and bring to the boil. Simmer, uncovered, stirring occasionally, for 15 minutes, or until the sauce has reduced and thickened. Return the pork to the wok and simmer for a further 5–10 minutes. Sprinkle with the oregano leaves.

Cook the pasta for 3–4 minutes until 'al dente' or according to packet directions, then drain and serve immediately with the pork and grated mozzarella cheese.

Try This: FOR AN ALTERNATIVE: 254   FOR A DIFFERENT MEAT OPTION: 158

Bacon, Mushroom & Cheese Puffs

SERVES 4

1 tbsp olive oil
225 g/8 oz field mushrooms,
   wiped and roughly chopped
225 g/8 oz rindless streaky
   bacon, roughly chopped
2 tbsp freshly chopped parsley

salt and freshly ground
   black pepper
350 g/12 oz ready-rolled puff
   pastry sheets, thawed
   if frozen
25 g/1 oz Emmenthal

cheese, grated
1 medium egg, beaten
salad leaves such as rocket
   or watercress, to garnish
tomatoes, to serve

Preheat the oven to 200°C/400°F/Gas Mark 6. Heat the olive oil in a large frying pan. Add the mushrooms and bacon and fry for 6–8 minutes until golden in colour. Stir in the parsley, season to taste with salt and pepper and allow to cool.

Roll the sheet of pastry a little thinner on a lightly floured surface to a 30.5 cm/12 inch square. Cut the pastry into 4 equal squares. Stir the grated Emmenthal cheese into the mushroom mixture. Spoon a quarter of the mixture on to one half of each square. Brush the edges of the square with a little of the beaten egg.

Fold over the pastry to form a triangular parcel. Seal the edges well and place on a lightly oiled baking sheet. Repeat until the squares are done.

Make shallow slashes in the top of the pastry with a knife. Brush the parcels with the remaining beaten egg and cook in the preheated oven for 20 minutes, or until puffy and golden brown.

Serve warm or cold, garnished with the salad leaves and served with tomatoes.

Try This: FOR AN ALTERNATIVE: 228 FOR A DIFFERENT MEAT OPTION: 320

Bacon & Tomato Breakfast Twist

SERVES 8

450 g/1 lb strong plain flour
½ tsp salt
7 g/¼ oz sachet easy-blend dried yeast
300 ml/½ pint warm milk
15 g/½ oz butter, melted

For the filling:
225 g/8 oz back bacon, derinded
15 g/½ oz butter, melted
175 g/6 oz ripe tomatoes, peeled, deseeded and chopped

freshly ground black pepper

To finish:
beaten egg, to glaze
2 tsp medium oatmeal

Preheat the oven to 200°C/400°F/Gas Mark 6, 15 minutes before baking. Sift the flour and salt into a large bowl. Stir in the yeast and make a well in the centre. Pour in the milk and butter and mix to a soft dough. Knead on a lightly floured surface for 10 minutes, until smooth and elastic. Put in an oiled bowl, cover with clingfilm and leave to rise in a warm place for 1 hour, until doubled in size.

Cook the bacon under a hot grill for 5–6 minutes, turning once, until crisp. Leave to cool, then roughly chop.

Knead the dough again for a minute or two. Roll it out to a 25.5 x 33 cm/10 x 13 inch rectangle. Cut in half lengthways. Lightly brush with butter, then scatter with the bacon, tomatoes and black pepper, leaving a 1 cm/½ inch margin around the edges. Brush the edges of the dough with beaten egg, then roll up each rectangle lengthways.

Place the 2 rolls side by side and twist together, pinching the ends to seal. Transfer to an oiled baking sheet and cover loosely with oiled clingfilm. Leave to rise in a warm place for 30 minutes. Brush with the beaten egg and sprinkle with the oatmeal. Bake in the preheated oven for about 30 minutes, or until golden brown and hollow-sounding when tapped on the base. Serve the bread warm in thick slices.

Try This: FOR AN ALTERNATIVE: 226   FOR A DIFFERENT MEAT OPTION: 300

Bacon & Split Pea Soup

SERVES 4

50 g/2 oz dried split peas
25 g/1 oz butter
1 garlic clove, peeled and finely chopped
1 medium onion, peeled and thinly sliced
175 g/6 oz long-grain rice

2 tbsp tomato purée
1.1 litres/2 pints vegetable or chicken stock
175 g/6 oz carrots, peeled and finely diced
125 g/4 oz streaky bacon, finely chopped

salt and freshly ground black pepper
2 tbsp freshly chopped parsley
4 tbsp single cream
warm crusty garlic bread, to serve

Cover the dried split peas with plenty of cold water, cover loosely and leave to soak for a minimum of 12 hours, preferably overnight.

Melt the butter in a heavy-based saucepan, add the garlic and onion and cook for 2–3 minutes, without colouring. Add the rice, drained split peas and tomato purée and cook for 2–3 minutes, stirring constantly to prevent sticking. Add the stock, bring to the boil, then reduce the heat and simmer for 20–25 minutes, or until the rice and peas are tender. Remove from the heat and leave to cool.

Blend about three-quarters of the soup in a food processor or blender to form a smooth purée. Pour the purée into the remaining soup in the saucepan. Add the carrots to the saucepan and cook for a further 10–12 minutes, or until the carrots are tender.

Meanwhile, place the bacon in a non-stick frying pan and cook over a gentle heat until the bacon is crisp. Remove and drain on absorbent kitchen paper.

Season the soup with salt and pepper to taste, then stir in the parsley and cream. Reheat for 2–3 minutes, then ladle into soup bowls. Sprinkle with the bacon and serve immediately with warm garlic bread.

Try This: FOR AN ALTERNATIVE: 246 FOR A DIFFERENT MEAT OPTION: 128

Jamaican Jerk Pork
with Rice & Peas

SERVES 4

175 g/6 oz dried red kidney
    beans, soaked overnight
2 onions, peeled and chopped
2 garlic cloves, peeled
    and crushed
4 tbsp lime juice
2 tbsp each dark molasses,
    soy sauce and chopped
    fresh root ginger
2 jalapeño chillies, deseeded

    and chopped
½ tsp ground cinnamon
¼ tsp each ground allspice,
    ground nutmeg
4 pork loin chops, on the bone

For the rice:
1 tbsp vegetable oil
1 onion, peeled and
    finely chopped

1 celery stalk, trimmed
    and finely sliced
3 garlic cloves, peeled
    and crushed
2 bay leaves
225 g/8 oz long-grain white rice
475 ml/18 fl oz chicken
    or ham stock
sprigs of fresh flat-leaf
    parsley, to garnish

To make the jerk pork marinade, purée the onions, garlic, lime juice, molasses, soy sauce, ginger, chillies, cinnamon, allspice and nutmeg together in a food processor until smooth. Put the pork chops into a plastic or non-reactive dish and pour over the marinade, turning the chops to coat. Marinate in the refrigerator for at least 1 hour or overnight.

Drain the beans and place in a large saucepan with about 2 litres/3½ pints cold water. Bring to the boil and boil rapidly for 10 minutes. Reduce the heat, cover and simmer gently, for 1 hour until tender, adding more water if necessary. When cooked, drain well and mash roughly.

Heat the oil for the rice in a saucepan with a tight-fitting lid and add the onion, celery and garlic. Cook gently for 5 minutes until softened. Add the bay leaves, rice and stock and stir. Bring to the boil, cover and cook very gently for 10 minutes. Add the beans and stir well again. Cook for a further 5 minutes, then remove from the heat.

Heat a griddle pan until almost smoking. Remove the pork chops from the marinade, scraping off any surplus and add to the hot pan. Cook for 5–8 minutes on each side, or until cooked. Garnish with the parsley and serve immediately with the rice.

Try This: FOR AN ALTERNATIVE: 210   FOR A DIFFERENT MEAT OPTION: 354

Pork Loin Stuffed with Orange & Hazelnut Rice

SERVES 4

15 g/½ oz butter
1 shallot, peeled and
    finely chopped
50 g/2 oz long-grain brown rice
175 ml/6 fl oz vegetable stock
½ orange
25 g/1 oz ready-to-eat

dried prunes, stoned
    and chopped
25 g/1 oz hazelnuts, roasted
    and roughly chopped
1 small egg, beaten
1 tbsp freshly chopped parsley
salt and freshly ground black

pepper
450 g/1 lb boneless pork
    tenderloin or fillet, trimmed

To serve:
steamed courgettes
carrots

Preheat the oven to 190˚C/375˚F/Gas Mark 5, 10 minutes before required. Heat the butter in a small saucepan, add the shallot and cook gently for 2–3 minutes until softened. Add the rice and stir well for 1 minute. Add the stock, stir well and bring to the boil. Cover tightly and simmer gently for 30 minutes until the rice is tender and all the liquid is absorbed. Leave to cool.

Grate the orange rind and reserve. Remove the white pith and chop the orange flesh finely. Mix together the orange rind and flesh, prunes, hazelnuts, cooled rice, egg and parsley. Season to taste with salt and pepper.

Cut the fillet in half, then using a sharp knife, split the pork fillet lengthways almost in two, forming a pocket, leaving it just attached. Open out the pork and put between 2 pieces of clingfilm. Flatten using a meat mallet until about half its original thickness. Spoon the filling into the pocket and close the fillet over. Tie along the length with kitchen string at regular intervals.

Put the pork fillet in a small roasting tray and cook in the top of the preheated oven for 25–30 minutes, or until the meat is just tender. Remove from the oven and allow to rest for 5 minutes. Slice into rounds and serve with steamed courgettes and carrots.

Try This: FOR AN ALTERNATIVE: 216   FOR A DIFFERENT MEAT OPTION: 326

Pork Goulash & Rice

SERVES 4

700 g/1½ lb boneless
   pork rib chops
1 tbsp olive oil
2 onions, peeled and
   roughly chopped
1 red pepper, deseeded
   and thinly sliced

1 garlic clove, peeled
   and crushed
1 tbsp plain flour
1 rounded tbsp paprika
400 g can chopped tomatoes
salt and freshly ground
   black pepper

250 g/9 oz long-grain
   white rice
450 ml/¾ pint chicken stock
sprigs of fresh flat-leaf
   parsley, to garnish
150 ml/¼ pint soured cream,
   to serve

Preheat the oven to 140°C/275°F/Gas Mark 1. Cut the pork into large cubes, about 4 cm/1½ inches square. Heat the oil in a large flameproof casserole and brown the pork in batches over a high heat, transferring the cubes to a plate as they brown.

Over a medium heat, add the onions and pepper and cook for about 5 minutes, stirring regularly, until they begin to brown. Add the garlic and return the meat to the casserole along with any juices on the plate. Sprinkle in the flour and paprika and stir well to soak up the oil and juices.

Add the tomatoes and season to taste with salt and pepper. Bring slowly to the boil, cover with a tight-fitting lid and cook in the preheated oven for 1½ hours.

Meanwhile, rinse the rice in several changes of water until the water remains relatively clear. Drain well and put into a saucepan with the chicken stock or water and a little salt. Cover tightly and bring to the boil. Turn the heat down as low as possible and cook for 10 minutes without removing the lid. After 10 minutes, remove from the heat and leave for a further 10 minutes, without removing the lid. Fluff with a fork.

When the meat is tender, stir in the soured cream lightly to create a marbled effect, or serve separately. Garnish with parsley and serve immediately with the rice.

    Try This: FOR AN ALTERNATIVE: 212 FOR A DIFFERENT MEAT OPTION: 68

Nasi Goreng

SERVES 4

7 large shallots, peeled
1 red chilli, deseeded and
    roughly chopped
2 garlic cloves, peeled and
    roughly chopped
4 tbsp sunflower oil
2 tsp each tomato purée and
    Indonesian sweet soy
    sauce (katjap manis)

225 g/8 oz long-grain
    white rice
125 g/4 oz French
    beans, trimmed
3 medium eggs, beaten
pinch of sugar
salt and freshly ground
    black pepper
225 g/8 oz cooked

ham, shredded
225 g/8 oz cooked peeled
    prawns, thawed if frozen
6 spring onions, trimmed
    and thinly sliced
1 tbsp light soy sauce
3 tbsp freshly
    chopped coriander

Roughly chop 1 of the shallots and place with the red chilli, garlic, 1 tablespoon of the oil, tomato purée and sweet soy sauce in a food processor and blend until smooth, then reserve. Boil the rice in plenty of salted water for 6–7 minutes until tender, adding the French beans after 4 minutes. Drain well and leave to cool. Beat the eggs with the sugar and a little salt and pepper. Heat a little of the oil in a small non-stick frying pan and add about one third of the egg mixture. Swirl to coat the base of the pan thinly and cook for about 1 minute until golden. Flip and cook the other side briefly before removing from the pan. Roll the omelette and slice thinly into strips. Repeat with the remaining egg to make 3 omelettes.

Thinly slice the remaining shallots then heat a further 2 tablespoons of the oil in a clean frying pan. Add the shallots to the pan and cook for 8–10 minutes over a medium heat until golden and crisp. Drain on absorbent kitchen paper and reserve. Add the remaining 1 tablespoon of oil to a large wok or frying pan and fry the chilli paste over a medium heat for 1 minute. Add the cooked rice and beans and stir-fry for 2 minutes. Add the ham and prawns and continue stir-frying for a further 1–2 minutes. Add the omelette slices, half the fried shallots, the spring onions, soy sauce and chopped coriander. Stir-fry for a further minute until heated through. Spoon on to serving plates and garnish with the remaining crispy shallots. Serve immediately.

Try This: FOR AN ALTERNATIVE: 200   FOR A DIFFERENT MEAT OPTION: 314

Leek & Ham Risotto

SERVES 4

1 tbsp olive oil
25 g/1 oz butter
1 medium onion, peeled
  and finely chopped
4 leeks, trimmed and
  thinly sliced

1½ tbsp freshly
  chopped thyme
350 g/12 oz Arborio rice
1.4 litres/2¼ pints vegetable
  or chicken stock, heated
225 g/8 oz cooked ham

175 g/6 oz peas, thawed
  if frozen
50 g/2 oz Parmesan
  cheese, grated
salt and freshly ground
  black pepper

Heat the oil and half the butter together in a large saucepan. Add the onion and leeks and cook over a medium heat for 6–8 minutes, stirring occasionally, until soft and beginning to colour. Stir in the thyme and cook briefly.

Add the rice and stir well. Continue stirring over a medium heat for about 1 minute until the rice is glossy. Add a ladleful or two of the stock and stir well until the stock is absorbed. Continue adding stock, a ladleful at a time, and stirring well between additions, until about two thirds of the stock has been added.

Meanwhile, either chop or finely shred the ham, then add to the saucepan of rice together with the peas. Continue adding ladlefuls of stock, as described in step 2, until the rice is tender and the ham is heated through thoroughly.

Add the remaining butter, sprinkle over the Parmesan cheese and season to taste with salt and pepper. When the butter has melted and the cheese has softened, stir well to incorporate. Taste and adjust the seasoning, then serve immediately.

Try This: FOR AN ALTERNATIVE: 212   FOR A DIFFERENT MEAT OPTION: 68

Pork Sausages with Onion Gravy & Best–ever Mash

SERVES 4

50 g/2 oz butter
1 tbsp olive oil
2 large onions, peeled
   and thinly sliced
pinch of sugar
1 tbsp freshly
   chopped thyme
1 tbsp plain flour

100 ml/3½ fl oz Madeira
200 ml/7 fl oz vegetable stock
8–12 good-quality butchers'
   pork sausages, depending
   on size

For the mash:
900 g/2 lb floury potatoes,
   peeled
75 g/3 oz butter
4 tbsp crème fraîche or
   soured cream
salt and freshly ground
   black pepper

Melt the butter with the oil and add the onions. Cover and cook gently for about 20 minutes until the onions have collapsed. Add the sugar and stir well. Uncover and continue to cook, stirring often, until the onions are very soft and golden. Add the thyme, stir well, then add the flour, stirring. Gradually add the Madeira and the stock. Bring to the boil and simmer gently for 10 minutes.

Meanwhile, put the sausages in a large frying pan and cook over a medium heat for about 15–20 minutes, turning often, until golden brown and slightly sticky all over.

For the mash, boil the potatoes in plenty of lightly salted water for 15–18 minutes until tender. Drain well and return to the saucepan. Put the saucepan over a low heat to allow the potatoes to dry thoroughly. Remove from the heat and add the butter, crème fraîche (or soured cream) and salt and pepper. Mash thoroughly. Serve the potato mash topped with the sausages and onion gravy.

Try This: FOR AN ALTERNATIVE: 254   FOR A DIFFERENT MEAT OPTION: 62

Roast Cured Pork Loin
with Baked Sliced Potatoes

SERVES 4

2 tbsp wholegrain mustard
2 tbsp clear honey
1 tsp coarsely crushed
  black pepper
900 g/2 lb piece smoked
  cured pork loin

900 g/2 lb potatoes, peeled
  and thinly sliced
75 g/3 oz butter, diced
1 large onion, peeled and
  finely chopped
25 g/1 oz plain flour

salt and freshly ground
  black pepper
600 ml/1 pint milk
fresh green salad, to serve

Preheat the oven to 190°C/375°F/Gas Mark 5. Mix together the mustard, honey and black pepper. Spread evenly over the pork loin. Place in the centre of a large square of foil and wrap loosely. Cook in the preheated oven for 15 minutes per 450 g/1 lb, plus an extra 15 minutes (45 minutes), unwrapping the joint for the last 30 minutes of cooking time.

Meanwhile, layer one third of the potatoes, one third of the butter, half the onions and half the flour in a large gratin dish. Add half the remaining potatoes and butter and the remaining onions and flour. Finally, cover with the remaining potatoes. Season well with salt and pepper between layers. Pour in the milk and dot with the remaining butter. Cover the dish loosely with foil and put in the oven below the pork. Cook for 1½ hours.

Remove the foil from the potatoes and cook for a further 20 minutes until tender and golden. Remove the pork loin from the oven and leave to rest for 10 minutes before carving thinly. Serve with the potatoes and a fresh green salad.

Try This: FOR AN ALTERNATIVE: 234 FOR A DIFFERENT MEAT OPTION: 66

Spanish–style Pork Stew with Saffron Rice

SERVES 4

2 tbsp olive oil
900 g/2 lb boneless pork
   shoulder, diced
1 large onion, peeled
   and sliced
2 garlic cloves, peeled and
   finely chopped
1 tbsp plain flour
450 g/1 lb plum tomatoes,
   peeled and chopped

175 ml/6 fl oz red wine
1 tbsp freshly chopped basil
1 green pepper, deseeded
   and sliced
50 g/2 oz pimiento-stuffed
   olives, cut in half crossways
salt and freshly ground
   black pepper
fresh basil leaves, to garnish

For the saffron rice:

1 tbsp olive oil
25 g/1 oz butter
1 small onion, peeled and
   finely chopped
few strands of saffron,
   crushed
250 g/9 oz long-grain
   white rice
600 ml/1 pint chicken stock

Preheat the oven to 150°C/300°F/Gas Mark 2. Heat the oil in a large flameproof casserole and add the pork in batches. Fry over a high heat until browned. Transfer to a plate until all the pork is browned.

Lower the heat and add the onion to the casserole. Cook for a further 5 minutes until soft and starting to brown. Add the garlic and stir briefly before returning the pork to the casserole. Add the flour and stir. Add the tomatoes. Gradually stir in the red wine and add the basil. Bring to simmering point and cover. Transfer the casserole to the lower part of the preheated oven and cook for 1½ hours. Stir in the green pepper and olives and cook for 30 minutes. Season to taste with salt and pepper.

Meanwhile, to make the saffron rice, heat the oil with the butter in a saucepan. Add the onion and cook for 5 minutes over a medium heat until softened. Add the saffron and rice and stir well. Add the stock, bring to the boil, cover and reduce the heat as low as possible. Cook for 15 minutes, covered, until the rice is tender and the stock is absorbed. Adjust the seasoning and serve with the stew, garnished with fresh basil.

Try This: FOR AN ALTERNATIVE: 230   FOR A DIFFERENT MEAT OPTION: 142

New Orleans Jambalaya

SERVES 6-8

For the seasoning mix:
2 dried bay leaves
1 tsp salt
2 tsp cayenne pepper, or to taste
2 tsp dried oregano
1 tsp each ground white and black pepper, or to taste
3 tbsp vegetable oil

125 g/4 oz ham, chopped
225 g/8 oz smoked pork sausage, cut into chunks
2 large onions, peeled and chopped
4 celery stalks, trimmed and chopped
2 green peppers, deseeded and chopped
2 garlic cloves, peeled

and finely chopped
350 g/12 oz raw chicken, diced
400 g can chopped tomatoes
600 ml/1 pint fish stock
400 g/14 oz long-grain white rice
4 spring onions, trimmed and coarsely chopped
275 g/10 oz raw prawns, peeled
250 g/9 oz white crab meat

Mix all the seasoning ingredients together in a small bowl and reserve. Heat 2 tablespoons of the oil in a large flameproof casserole over a medium heat. Add the ham and sausage and cook, stirring often, for 7–8 minutes until golden. Remove from the pan and reserve.

Add the remaining onions, celery and peppers to the casserole and cook for about 4 minutes, or until softened, stirring occasionally. Stir in the garlic then, using a slotted spoon, transfer all the vegetables to a plate and reserve with the sausage.

Add the chicken pieces to the casserole and cook for about 4 minutes, or until beginning to colour, turning once. Stir in the seasoning mix and turn the pieces to coat well. Return the sausage and vegetables to the casserole and stir well. Add the chopped tomatoes, with their juice, and the stock and bring to the boil.

Stir in the rice and reduce the heat to low. Cover and simmer for 12 minutes. Uncover, stir in the spring onions and prawns and cook, covered, for a further 4 minutes. Add the crab and gently stir in. Cook for 2–3 minutes, or until the rice is tender. Remove from the heat, cover and leave to stand for 5 minutes before serving.

Try This: FOR AN ALTERNATIVE: 212   FOR A DIFFERENT MEAT OPTION: 322

Chinese–style Fried Rice

SERVES 4–6

2–3 tbsp groundnut oil
   or vegetable oil
2 small onions, peeled
   and cut into wedges
2 garlic cloves, peeled
   and thinly sliced
2.5 cm/1 inch piece fresh
   root ginger, peeled and
   cut into thin slivers
225 g/8 oz cooked chicken,
   thinly sliced
125 g/4 oz cooked ham,
thinly sliced
350 g/12 oz cooked cold
   long-grain white rice
125 g/4 oz canned water
   chestnuts, sliced
225 g/8 oz cooked peeled
   prawns (optional)
3 large eggs
3 tsp sesame oil
salt and freshly ground
   black pepper
6 spring onions, trimmed
and sliced into 1 cm/½
   inch pieces
2 tbsp dark soy sauce
1 tbsp sweet chilli sauce
2 tbsp freshly chopped
   coriander

To garnish:
2 tbsp chopped
   roasted peanuts
sprig of fresh coriander

Heat a wok or large deep frying pan until very hot, add the oil and heat for 30 seconds. Add the onions and stir-fry for 2 minutes. Stir in the garlic and ginger and cook for 1 minute. Add the cooked sliced chicken and ham and stir-fry for a further 2–3 minutes.

Add the rice, the water chestnuts and prawns, if using, with 2 tablespoons of water and stir-fry for 2 minutes until the rice is heated through.

Beat the eggs with 1 teaspoon of the sesame oil and season to taste with salt and pepper. Make a well in the centre of the rice, then pour in the egg mixture and stir immediately, gradually drawing the rice mixture into the egg, until the egg is cooked.

Add the spring onions, soy and chilli sauces, coriander and a little water, if necessary. Adjust the seasoning and drizzle with the remaining sesame oil. Sprinkle with the nuts and serve.

Try This: FOR AN ALTERNATIVE: 200   FOR A DIFFERENT MEAT OPTION: 326

Tagliatelle with Stuffed Pork Escalopes

SERVES 4

150 g/5 oz broccoli florets, finely chopped and blanched
125 g/4 oz mozzarella cheese, grated
1 garlic clove, peeled and crushed

2 large eggs, beaten
salt and freshly ground black pepper
4 thin pork escalopes, weighing about 100 g/ 3½ oz each
1 tbsp olive oil

25 g/1 oz butter
2 tbsp flour
150 ml/¼ pint milk
150 ml/¼ pint chicken stock
1 tbsp Dijon mustard
225 g/8 oz fresh tagliatelle
sage leaves, to garnish

Preheat the oven to 180°C/350°F/Gas Mark 4, 10 minutes before cooking. Mix the broccoli with the mozzarella cheese, garlic and beaten eggs. Season to taste with salt and pepper and reserve.

Using a meat mallet or rolling pin, pound the escalopes on a sheet of greaseproof paper until 5 mm/¼ inch thick. Divide the broccoli mixture between the escalopes and roll each one up from the shortest side. Place the pork rolls in a lightly oiled ovenproof dish, drizzle over the olive oil and bake in the preheated oven for 40–50 minutes, or until cooked.

Meanwhile, melt the butter in a heavy-based pan, stir in the flour and cook for 2 minutes. Remove from the heat and whisk in the milk and stock. Season to taste, stir in the mustard then cook until smooth and thickened. Keep warm.

Bring a large pan of lightly salted water to a rolling boil. Add the tagliatelle and cook according to the packet instructions, about 3–4 minutes, or until 'al dente'. Drain thoroughly and tip into a warmed serving dish. Slice each pork roll into 3, place on top of the pasta and pour the sauce over. Garnish with sage leaves and serve immediately.

Try This: FOR AN ALTERNATIVE: 176   FOR A DIFFERENT MEAT OPTION: 164

Oven–roasted Vegetables with Sausages

SERVES 4

2 medium aubergines, trimmed
3 medium courgettes, trimmed
4 tbsp olive oil

6 garlic cloves, peeled
8 Tuscany-style sausages
4 plum tomatoes
2 x 300 g cans cannellini beans
salt and freshly ground

black pepper
1 bunch of fresh basil, torn into coarse pieces
4 tbsp Parmesan cheese, grated

Preheat oven to 200°C/400°F/Gas Mark 6, 15 minutes before cooking. Cut the aubergines and courgettes into bite-sized chunks. Place the olive oil in a large roasting tin and heat in the preheated oven for 3 minutes, or until very hot. Add the aubergines, courgettes and garlic cloves, then stir until coated in the hot oil and cook in the oven for 10 minutes.

Remove the roasting tin from the oven and stir. Lightly prick the sausages, add to the roasting tin and return to the oven. Continue to roast for a further 20 minutes, turning once during cooking, until the vegetables are tender and the sausages are golden brown.

Meanwhile, roughly chop the plum tomatoes and drain the cannellini beans. Remove the sausages from the oven and stir in the tomatoes and cannellini beans. Season to taste with salt and pepper, then return to the oven for 5 minutes, or until heated thoroughly.

Scatter over the basil leaves and sprinkle with plenty of Parmesan cheese and extra freshly ground black pepper. Serve immediately.

Try This: FOR AN ALTERNATIVE: 262   FOR A DIFFERENT MEAT OPTION: 366

Hot Salami & Vegetable Gratin

SERVES 4

350 g/12 oz carrots
175 g/6 oz fine green beans
250 g/9 oz asparagus tips
175 g/6 oz frozen peas
225 g/8 oz Italian salami
1 tbsp olive oil

1 tbsp freshly chopped mint
25 g/1 oz butter
150 g/5 oz baby spinach leaves
150 ml/¼ pint double cream
salt and freshly ground
    black pepper

1 small or ½ an olive ciabatta
    loaf
75 g/3 oz Parmesan
    cheese, grated
green salad, to serve

Preheat oven to 200°C/400°F/Gas Mark 6. Peel and slice the carrots, trim the beans and asparagus and reserve. Cook the carrots in a saucepan of lightly salted, boiling water for 5 minutes. Add the remaining vegetables, except the spinach, and cook for about a further 5 minutes, or until tender. Drain and place in an ovenproof dish.

Discard any skin from the outside of the salami, if necessary, then chop roughly. Heat the oil in a frying pan and fry the salami for 4–5 minutes, stirring occasionally, until golden. Using a slotted spoon, transfer the salami to the ovenproof dish and scatter over the mint.

Add the butter to the frying pan and cook the spinach for 1–2 minutes, or until just wilted. Stir in the double cream and season well with salt and pepper. Spoon the mixture over the vegetables.

Whiz the ciabatta loaf in a food processor to make breadcrumbs. Stir in the Parmesan cheese and sprinkle over the vegetables. Bake in the preheated oven for 20 minutes, until golden and heated through. Serve with a green salad.

Try This: FOR AN ALTERNATIVE: 276   FOR A DIFFERENT MEAT OPTION: 332

Antipasto Penne

SERVES 4

3 medium courgettes, trimmed
4 plum tomatoes
175 g/6 oz Italian ham
2 tbsp olive oil

salt and freshly ground black pepper
350 g/12 oz dried penne pasta
285 g jar antipasto
125 g/4 oz mozzarella

cheese, drained and diced
125 g/4 oz Gorgonzola cheese, crumbled
3 tbsp freshly chopped flat-leaf parsley

Preheat the grill just before cooking. Cut the courgettes into thick slices. Rinse the tomatoes and cut into quarters, then cut the ham into strips. Pour the oil into a baking dish and place under the grill for 2 minutes, or until almost smoking. Remove from the grill and stir in the courgettes. Return to the grill and cook for 8 minutes, stirring occasionally. Remove from the grill and add the tomatoes and cook for a further 3 minutes.

Add the ham to the baking dish and cook under the grill for 4 minutes, until all the vegetables are charred and the ham is brown. Season to taste with salt and pepper.

Meanwhile, plunge the pasta into a large saucepan of lightly salted, boiling water, return to a rolling boil, stir and cook for 8 minutes, or until 'al dente'. Drain well and return to the saucepan.

Stir the antipasto into the vegetables and cook under the grill for 2 minutes, or until heated through. Add the cooked pasta and toss together gently with the remaining ingredients. Grill for a further 4 minutes, then serve immediately.

Try This: FOR AN ALTERNATIVE: 270 FOR A DIFFERENT MEAT OPTION: 158

Italian Risotto

SERVES 4

1 onion, peeled
2 garlic cloves, peeled
1 tbsp olive oil
125 g/4 oz Italian salami
    or speck, chopped
125 g/4 oz asparagus
350 g/12 oz risotto rice

300 ml/½ pt dry white wine
1 litre/1¾ pints chicken stock,
    warmed
125g/4 oz frozen broad
    beans, defrosted
125g/4 oz Dolcelatte
    cheese, diced

3 tbsp freshly chopped
    mixed herbs, such as
    parsley and basil
salt and freshly ground
    black pepper

Chop the onion and garlic and reserve. Heat the olive oil in a large frying pan and cook the salami for 3–5 minutes, or until golden. Using a slotted spoon, transfer to a plate and keep warm. Add the asparagus and stir-fry for 2–3 minutes, until just wilted. Transfer to the plate with the salami. Add the onion and garlic and cook for 5 minutes, or until softened.

Add the rice to the pan and cook for about 2 minutes. Add the wine, bring to the boil, then simmer, stirring until the wine has been absorbed. Add half the stock and return to the boil. Simmer, stirring, until the liquid has been absorbed.

Add half of the remaining stock and the broad beans to the rice mixture. Bring to the boil, then simmer for a further 5–10 minutes, or until all of the liquid has been absorbed.

Add the remaining stock, bring to the boil, then simmer until all the liquid is absorbed and the rice is tender. Stir in the remaining ingredients until the cheese has just melted. Serve immediately.

Try This: FOR AN ALTERNATIVE: 240   FOR A DIFFERENT MEAT OPTION: 68

Oven–baked Pork Balls with Peppers

SERVES 4

For the garlic bread:
2–4 garlic cloves, peeled
50 g/2 oz butter, softened
1 tbsp freshly chopped parsley
2–3 tsp lemon juice
1 focaccia loaf

For the pork balls:
450 g/1 lb fresh pork mince
4 tbsp freshly chopped basil

2 garlic cloves, peeled
   and chopped
3 sun-dried tomatoes,
   chopped
salt and freshly ground
   black pepper
3 tbsp olive oil
1 medium red pepper,
   deseeded and cut
   into chunks

1 medium green pepper,
   deseeded and cut
   into chunks
1 medium yellow pepper,
   deseeded and cut
   into chunks
225 g/8 oz cherry tomatoes
2 tbsp balsamic vinegar

Preheat oven to 200°C/400°F/Gas Mark 6, 15 minutes before cooking. Crush the garlic, then blend with the softened butter, the parsley and enough lemon juice to give a soft consistency. Shape into a roll, wrap in baking parchment and chill in the refrigerator for at least 30 minutes.

Mix together the pork, basil, 1 chopped garlic clove, sun-dried tomatoes and seasoning until well combined. With damp hands, divide the mixture into 16, roll into balls and reserve.

Spoon the olive oil in a large roasting tin and place in the preheated oven for about 3 minutes, or until very hot. Remove from the heat and stir in the pork balls, the remaining chopped garlic and peppers. Bake for about 15 minutes. Remove from the oven and stir in the cherry tomatoes and season to taste with plenty of salt and pepper. Bake for about a further 20 minutes.

Just before the pork balls are ready, slice the bread, toast lightly and spread with the prepared garlic butter. Remove the pork balls from the oven, stir in the vinegar and serve immediately with garlic bread.

Try This: FOR AN ALTERNATIVE: 190   FOR A DIFFERENT MEAT OPTION: 76

Pork Chop Hotpot

SERVES 4

4 pork chops
flour for dusting
225 g/8 oz shallots, peeled
2 garlic cloves, peeled
50 g/2 oz sun-dried tomatoes
2 tbsp olive oil
400 g can plum tomatoes

150 ml/¼ pint red wine
150 ml/¼ pint chicken stock
3 tbsp tomato purée
2 tbsp freshly
   chopped oregano
salt and freshly ground
   black pepper

fresh oregano leaves,
   to garnish

To serve:
freshly cooked new potatoes
French beans

Preheat oven to 190°C/375°F/Gas Mark 5, 10 minutes before cooking. Trim the pork chops, removing any excess fat, wipe with a clean, damp cloth, then dust with a little flour and reserve. Cut the shallots in half if large. Chop the garlic and slice the sun-dried tomatoes.

Heat the olive oil in a large casserole and cook the pork chops for about 5 minutes, turning occasionally during cooking, until browned all over. Using a slotted spoon, carefully lift out of the dish and reserve. Add the shallots and cook for 5 minutes, stirring occasionally.

Return the pork chops to the casserole and scatter with the garlic and sun-dried tomatoes, then pour over the can of tomatoes with their juice.

Blend the red wine, stock and tomato purée together and add the chopped oregano. Season to taste with salt and pepper, then pour over the pork chops and bring to a gentle boil. Cover with a close-fitting lid and cook in the preheated oven for 1 hour, or until the pork chops are tender. Adjust the seasoning to taste, then scatter with a few oregano leaves and serve immediately with freshly cooked potatoes and French beans.

Try This: FOR AN ALTERNATIVE: 236   FOR A DIFFERENT MEAT OPTION: 142

Cannelloni

SERVES 4

2 tbsp olive oil
175 g/6 oz fresh pork mince
75 g/3 oz chicken livers, chopped
1 small onion, peeled and chopped
1 garlic clove, peeled and chopped

175 g/6 oz frozen chopped spinach, thawed
1 tbsp freeze-dried oregano
pinch of freshly grated nutmeg
salt and freshly ground black pepper
175 g/6 oz ricotta cheese
25 g/1 oz butter

25 g/1 oz plain flour
600 ml/1 pint milk
600 ml/1 pint ready-made tomato sauce
16 precooked cannelloni tubes
50 g/2 oz Parmesan cheese, grated
green salad, to serve

Preheat oven to 190°C/375°F/Gas Mark 5, 10 minutes before cooking. Heat the olive oil in a frying pan and cook the mince and chicken livers for about 5 minutes, stirring occasionally, until browned all over. Break up any lumps if necessary with a wooden spoon.

Add the onion and garlic and cook for 4 minutes, until softened. Add the spinach, oregano and nutmeg and season to taste with salt and pepper. Cook until all the liquid has evaporated, then remove the pan from the heat and allow to cool. Stir in the ricotta cheese.

Meanwhile, melt the butter in a small saucepan and stir in the plain flour to form a roux. Cook for 2 minutes, stirring occasionally. Remove from the heat and blend in the milk until smooth. Return to the heat and bring to the boil, stirring until the sauce has thickened. Reserve.

Spoon a thin layer of the tomato sauce on the base of a large ovenproof dish. Divide the pork filling between the cannelloni tubes. Arrange on top of the tomato sauce. Spoon over the remaining tomato sauce.

Pour over the white sauce and sprinkle with the Parmesan cheese. Bake in the preheated oven for 30–35 minutes, or until the cannelloni is tender and the top is golden brown. Serve immediately with a green salad.

Try This: FOR AN ALTERNATIVE: 272   FOR A DIFFERENT MEAT OPTION: 362

Chorizo with Pasta in a Tomato Sauce

SERVES 4

25 g/1 oz butter
2 tbsp olive oil
2 large onions, peeled and finely sliced
1 tsp soft brown sugar
2 garlic cloves, peeled

and crushed
225 g/8 oz chorizo, sliced
1 chilli, deseeded and finely sliced
400 g can chopped tomatoes
1 tbsp sun-dried tomato paste

150 ml/¼ pint red wine
salt and freshly ground black pepper
450 g/1 lb rigatoni
freshly chopped parsley, to garnish

Melt the butter with the olive oil in a large heavy-based pan. Add the onions and sugar and cook over a very low heat, stirring occasionally, for 15 minutes, or until soft and starting to caramelize.

Add the garlic and chorizo to the pan and cook for 5 minutes. Stir in the chilli, chopped tomatoes and tomato paste, and pour in the wine. Season well with salt and pepper. Bring to the boil, cover, reduce the heat and simmer for 30 minutes, stirring occasionally. Remove the lid and simmer for a further 10 minutes, or until the sauce starts to thicken.

Meanwhile, bring a large pan of lightly salted water to a rolling boil. Add the pasta and cook according to the packet instructions, or until 'al dente'.

Drain the pasta, reserving 2 tablespoons of the water, and return to the pan. Add the chorizo sauce with the reserved cooking water and toss gently until the pasta is evenly covered. Tip into a warmed serving dish, sprinkle with the parsley and serve immediately.

Try This: FOR AN ALTERNATIVE: 280   FOR A DIFFERENT MEAT OPTION: 362

Pasta & Pork Ragù

SERVES 4

1 tbsp sunflower oil
1 leek, trimmed and
    thinly sliced
225 g/8 oz pork fillet, diced
1 garlic clove, peeled
    and crushed
2 tsp paprika

¼ tsp cayenne pepper
150 ml/¼ pint white wine
600 ml/1 pint vegetable stock
400 g can borlotti beans,
    drained and rinsed
2 carrots, peeled and diced
salt and freshly ground

black pepper
225 g/8 oz fresh egg tagliatelle
1 tbsp freshly chopped
    parsley, to garnish
crème fraîche, to serve

Heat the sunflower oil in a large frying pan. Add the sliced leek and cook, stirring frequently, for 5 minutes, or until softened. Add the pork and cook, stirring, for 4 minutes, or until sealed.

Add the crushed garlic, the paprika and cayenne pepper to the pan and stir until all the pork is lightly coated in the garlic and pepper mixture.

Pour in the wine and 450 ml/¾ pint of the vegetable stock. Add the borlotti beans and carrots and season to taste with salt and pepper. Bring the sauce to the boil, then lower the heat and simmer for 5 minutes.

Meanwhile, place the egg tagliatelle in a large saucepan of lightly salted, boiling water, cover and simmer for 5 minutes, or until the pasta is cooked 'al dente'.

Drain the pasta, then add to the pork ragù; toss well. Adjust the seasoning, then tip into a warmed serving dish. Sprinkle with chopped parsley and serve with a little crème fraîche.

Try This: FOR AN ALTERNATIVE: 258   FOR A DIFFERENT MEAT OPTION: 108

Sausage & Redcurrant Pasta Bake

SERVES 4

450 g/1 lb good quality,
thick pork sausages
2 tsp sunflower oil
25 g/1 oz butter
1 onion, peeled and sliced
2 tbsp plain white flour
450 ml/¾ pint chicken stock

150 ml/¼ pint port or good
quality red wine
1 tbsp freshly chopped
thyme leaves, plus
sprigs to garnish
1 bay leaf
4 tbsp redcurrant jelly

salt and freshly ground
black pepper
350 g/12 oz fresh penne
75 g/3 oz Gruyère
cheese, grated

Preheat the oven to 220°C/425°F/Gas Mark 7, 15 minutes before cooking. Prick the sausages, place in a shallow ovenproof dish and toss in the sunflower oil. Cook in the oven for 25–30 minutes, or until golden brown.

Meanwhile, melt the butter in a frying pan, add the sliced onion and fry for 5 minutes, or until golden brown. Stir in the flour and cook for 2 minutes. Remove the pan from the heat and gradually stir in the chicken stock with the port or red wine.

Return the pan to the heat and bring to the boil, stirring continuously until the sauce starts to thicken. Add the thyme, bay leaf and redcurrant jelly and season well with salt and pepper. Simmer the sauce for 5 minutes.

Bring a large pan of salted water to a rolling boil, add the pasta and cook for about 4 minutes, or until 'al dente'. Drain thoroughly and reserve.

Lower the oven temperature to 200°C/400°F/Gas Mark 6. Remove the sausages from the oven, drain off any excess fat and return the sausages to the dish. Add the pasta. Pour over the sauce, removing the bay leaf, and toss together. Sprinkle with the Gruyère cheese and return to the oven for 15–20 minutes, or until bubbling and golden brown. Serve immediately, garnished with thyme sprigs.

Try This: FOR AN ALTERNATIVE: 278   FOR A DIFFERENT MEAT OPTION: 152

Pappardelle Pork
with Brandy Sauce

SERVES 4

4 pork fillets, each weighing
  about 175 g/6 oz
1 tbsp freshly chopped sage,
  plus whole leaves to
  garnish
salt and freshly ground

black pepper
4 slices Parma ham
1 tbsp olive oil
6 tbsp brandy
300 ml/½ pint chicken stock
200 ml/7 fl oz double cream

350 g/12 oz pappardelle
1–2 tsp butter
2 tbsp freshly chopped
  flat-leaf parsley

Preheat the oven to 200°C/400°F/Gas Mark 6, 15 minutes before cooking. Using a sharp knife, cut two slits in each pork fillet then stuff each slit with chopped sage. Season well with salt and pepper and wrap each fillet with a slice of Parma ham.

Heat the olive oil in a large frying pan. Add the wrapped pork fillets and cook, turning once, for 1–2 minutes, or until the Parma ham is golden brown. Transfer to a roasting tin and cook in the preheated oven for 10–12 minutes.

Return the frying pan to the heat and add the brandy, scraping the bottom of the pan with a spoon to release all the flavours. Boil for 1 minute, then pour in the chicken stock. Boil for a further 2 minutes then pour in the cream and boil again for 2–3 minutes, or until the sauce has thickened slightly. Season the brandy sauce to taste.

Bring a large pan of lightly salted water to a rolling boil. Add the pasta and cook according to the packet instructions, or until 'al dente'. Drain the pasta thoroughly and return to the pan. Add the butter and chopped parsley and toss together. Keep the pasta warm.

Remove the pork from the oven and pour any juices into the brandy sauce. Pile the pasta on to individual plates, season with pepper, spoon over the brandy sauce and serve immediately with the pork fillets.

Try This: FOR AN ALTERNATIVE: 280 FOR A DIFFERENT MEAT OPTION: 372

Tagliatelle with
Spicy Sausage Ragù

SERVES 4

3 tbsp olive oil
6 spicy sausages
1 small onion, peeled and
   finely chopped
1 tsp fennel seeds
175 g/6 oz fresh pork mince

225 g can chopped tomatoes
   with garlic
1 tbsp sun-dried tomato paste
2 tbsp red wine or port
salt and freshly ground
   black pepper

350 g/12 oz tagliatelle
300 ml/½ pint prepared
   white sauce (bought or
   see page 266)
50 g/2 oz freshly grated
   Parmesan cheese

Preheat the oven to 200˚C/400˚F/Gas Mark 6, 15 minutes before cooking. Heat 1 tablespoon of the olive oil in a large frying pan. Prick the sausages, add to the pan and cook for 8–10 minutes, or until browned and cooked through. Remove and cut into thin diagonal slices. Reserve.

Return the pan to the heat and pour in the remaining olive oil. Add the onion and cook for 8 minutes, or until softened. Add the fennel seeds and minced pork and cook, stirring, for 5–8 minutes, or until the meat is sealed and browned.

Stir in the tomatoes, tomato paste and the wine or port. Season to taste with salt and pepper. Bring to the boil, cover and simmer for 30 minutes, stirring occasionally. Remove the lid and simmer for 10 minutes.

Bring a large pan of lightly salted water to a rolling boil. Add the pasta and cook according to the packet instructions, or until 'al dente'. Drain thoroughly and toss with the meat sauce.

Place half the pasta in an ovenproof dish, and cover with 4 tablespoons of the white sauce. Top with half the sausages and grated Parmesan cheese. Repeat the layering, finishing with white sauce and Parmesan cheese. Bake in the preheated oven for 20 minutes, until golden brown. Serve immediately.

Try This: FOR AN ALTERNATIVE: 212   FOR A DIFFERENT MEAT OPTION: 164

Gnocchi & Parma Ham Bake

SERVES 4

3 tbsp olive oil
1 red onion, peeled and sliced
2 garlic cloves, peeled
175 g/6 oz plum tomatoes,
    skinned and quartered
2 tbsp sun-dried tomato paste
250 g tub mascarpone cheese

salt and freshly ground
    black pepper
1 tbsp freshly chopped
    tarragon
300 g/11 oz fresh gnocchi
125 g/4 oz Cheddar or
    Parmesan cheese, grated

50 g/2 oz fresh white
    breadcrumbs
50 g/2 oz Parma ham, sliced
10 pitted green olives, halved
sprigs of flat-leaf parsley.
    to garnish

Heat the oven to 180°C/350°F/Gas Mark 4, 10 minutes before cooking. Heat 2 tablespoons of the olive oil in a large frying pan and cook the onion and garlic for 5 minutes, or until softened. Stir in the tomatoes, sun-dried tomato paste and mascarpone cheese. Season to taste with salt and pepper. Add half the tarragon. Bring to the boil, then lower the heat immediately and simmer for 5 minutes.

Meanwhile, bring 1.7 litres/3 pints water to the boil in a large pan. Add the remaining olive oil and a good pinch of salt. Add the gnocchi and cook for 1–2 minutes, or until they rise to the surface.

Drain the gnocchi thoroughly and transfer to a large ovenproof dish. Add the tomato sauce and toss gently to coat the pasta. Combine the Cheddar or Parmesan cheese with the breadcrumbs and remaining tarragon and scatter over the pasta mixture. Top with the Parma ham and olives and season again.

Cook in the preheated oven for 20–25 minutes, or until golden and bubbling. Serve immediately, garnished with parsley sprigs.

Try This: FOR AN ALTERNATIVE: 272   FOR A DIFFERENT MEAT OPTION: 108

Gammon with Red Wine Sauce & Pasta

SERVES 2

25 g/1 oz butter
150 ml/¼ pint red wine
4 red onions, peeled
   and sliced
4 tbsp orange juice

1 tsp soft brown sugar
225 g/8 oz gammon
   steak, trimmed
freshly ground black pepper
175 g/6 oz fusilli

3 tbsp wholegrain mustard
2 tbsp freshly chopped flat-
   leaf parsley, plus sprigs
   to garnish

Preheat the grill to a medium heat before cooking. Heat the butter with the red wine in a large heavy-based pan. Add the onions, cover with a tight-fitting lid and cook over a very low heat for 30 minutes, or until softened and transparent. Remove the lid from the pan, stir in the orange juice and sugar, then increase the heat and cook for about 10 minutes, until the onions are golden.

Meanwhile, cook the gammon steak under the preheated grill, turning at least once, for 4–6 minutes, or until tender. Cut the cooked gammon into bite-sized pieces. Reserve and keep warm.

Meanwhile, bring a large pan of very lightly salted water to a rolling boil. Add the pasta and cook according to the packet instructions, or until 'al dente'. Drain the pasta thoroughly, return to the pan, season with a little pepper and keep warm.

Stir the wholegrain mustard and chopped parsley into the onion sauce then pour over the pasta. Add the gammon pieces to the pan and toss lightly to thoroughly coat the pasta with the sauce. Pile the pasta mixture on to 2 warmed serving plates. Garnish with sprigs of flat-leaf parsley and serve immediately.

Try This: FOR AN ALTERNATIVE: 258   FOR A DIFFERENT MEAT OPTION: 146

Prosciutto & Gruyère Carbonara

SERVES 4

3 medium egg yolks
50 g/2 oz Gruyère
  cheese, grated
2 tbsp olive oil
2 garlic cloves, peeled
  and crushed

2 shallots, peeled and
  finely chopped
200 g/7 oz prosciutto ham,
  cut into strips
4 tbsp dry vermouth
salt and freshly ground

black pepper
450 g/1 lb spaghetti
15 g/½ oz butter
1 tbsp freshly shredded
  basil leaves
basil sprigs, to garnish

Place the egg yolks with 6 tablespoons of the Gruyère cheese in a bowl and mix lightly until well blended, then reserve.

Heat the olive oil in a large pan and cook the garlic and shallots for 5 minutes, or until golden brown. Add the prosciutto ham, then cook for a further 1 minute. Pour in the dry vermouth and simmer for 2 minutes, then remove from the heat. Season to taste with salt and pepper and keep warm.

Meanwhile, bring a large pan of lightly salted water to a rolling boil. Add the pasta and cook according to the packet instructions, or until 'al dente'. Drain thoroughly, reserving 4 tablespoons of the water, and return the pasta to the pan.

Remove from the heat, then add the egg and cheese mixture with the butter to the pasta; toss lightly until coated. Add the prosciutto mixture and toss again, adding the reserved pasta water, if needed, to moisten. Season to taste and sprinkle with the remaining Gruyère cheese and the shredded basil leaves. Garnish with basil sprigs and serve immediately.

Try This: FOR AN ALTERNATIVE: 226   FOR A DIFFERENT MEAT OPTION: 364

Poultry & Game

Clear Chicken & Mushroom Soup

SERVES 4

2 large chicken legs, about
    450 g/1 lb total weight
1 tbsp groundnut oil
1 tsp sesame oil
1 onion, peeled and
    very thinly sliced
2.5 cm/1 inch piece root
    ginger, peeled and

very finely chopped
1.1 litres/2 pints clear
    chicken stock
1 lemon grass stalk, bruised
50 g/2 oz long-grain rice
75 g/3 oz button
    mushrooms, wiped
    and finely sliced

4 spring onions, trimmed,
    cut into 5 cm/2 inch pieces
    and shredded
1 tbsp dark soy sauce
4 tbsp dry sherry
salt and freshly ground
    black pepper

Skin the chicken legs and remove any fat. Cut each in half to make 2 thigh and 2 drumstick portions and reserve. Heat the groundnut and sesame oils in a large saucepan. Add the sliced onion and cook gently for 10 minutes, or until soft but not beginning to colour.

Add the chopped ginger to the saucepan and cook for about 30 seconds, stirring all the time to prevent it sticking, then pour in the stock. Add the chicken pieces and the lemon grass, cover and simmer gently for 15 minutes. Stir in the rice and cook for a further 15 minutes or until the chicken is cooked.

Remove the chicken from the saucepan and leave until cool enough to handle. Finely shred the flesh, then return to the saucepan with the mushrooms, spring onions, soy sauce and sherry. Simmer for 5 minutes, or until the rice and mushrooms are tender. Remove the lemon grass.

Season the soup to taste with salt and pepper. Ladle into warmed serving bowls, making sure each has an equal amount of shredded chicken and vegetables and serve immediately.

Try This: FOR AN ALTERNATIVE: 288   FOR A DIFFERENT MEAT OPTION: 230

Creamy Caribbean Chicken & Coconut Soup

SERVES 4

6–8 spring onions
2 garlic cloves
1 red chilli
175 g/6 oz cooked chicken,
    shredded or diced
2 tbsp vegetable oil
1 tsp ground turmeric

300 ml/½ pint coconut milk
900 ml/1½ pints chicken stock
50 g/2 oz small soup pasta
    or spaghetti, broken into
    small pieces
½ lemon, sliced
salt and freshly ground

black pepper
1–2 tbsp freshly
    chopped coriander
sprigs of fresh coriander,
    to garnish

Trim the spring onions and slice thinly; peel the garlic and chop finely. Cut off the top from the chilli, slit down the side and remove seeds and membrane, then chop finely and reserve.

Remove and discard any skin or bones from the cooked chicken and shred using 2 forks and reserve.

Heat a large wok, add the oil and when hot, add the spring onions, garlic and chilli and stir-fry for 2 minutes, or until the onion has softened. Stir in the turmeric and cook for 1 minute.

Blend the coconut milk with the chicken stock until smooth, then pour into the wok. Add the pasta or spaghetti with the lemon slices and bring to the boil.

Simmer, half covered, for 10–12 minutes, or until the pasta is tender; stir occasionally.

Remove the lemon slices from the wok and add the chicken. Season to taste with salt and pepper and simmer for 2–3 minutes, or until the chicken is heated through thoroughly.

Stir in the chopped coriander and ladle into heated bowls. Garnish with sprigs of fresh coriander and serve immediately.

Try This: FOR AN ALTERNATIVE: 286   FOR A DIFFERENT MEAT OPTION: 194

Chicken Noodle Soup

SERVES 4

carcass of a medium-sized cooked chicken
1 large carrot, peeled and roughly chopped
1 medium onion, peeled and quartered
1 leek, trimmed and

roughly chopped
2–3 bay leaves
a few black peppercorns
2 litres/3½ pints water
225 g/8 oz Chinese cabbage, trimmed
50 g/2 oz chestnut

mushrooms, wiped and sliced
125 g/4 oz cooked chicken, sliced or chopped
50 g/2 oz medium or fine egg thread noodles

Break the chicken carcass into smaller pieces and place in the wok with the carrot, onion, leek, bay leaves, peppercorns and water. Bring slowly to the boil. Skim away any fat or scum that rises for the first 15 minutes. Simmer very gently for 1–1½ hours. If the liquid reduces by more than one third, add a little more water.

Remove from the heat and leave until cold. Strain into a large bowl and chill in the refrigerator until any fat in the stock rises and sets on the surface. Remove the fat and discard. Draw a sheet of absorbent kitchen paper across the surface of the stock to absorb any remaining fat.

Return the stock to the wok and bring to a simmer. Add the Chinese cabbage, mushrooms and chicken and simmer gently for 7–8 minutes until the vegetables are tender.

Meanwhile, cook the noodles according to the packet instructions until tender. Drain well. Transfer a portion of noodles to each serving bowl before pouring in some soup and vegetables. Serve immediately.

Try This: FOR AN ALTERNATIVE: 286 FOR A DIFFERENT MEAT OPTION: 178

Chicken–filled Spring Rolls

MAKES 12–14 ROLLS

For the filling:
1 tbsp vegetable oil
2 slices streaky bacon, diced
225 g/8 oz skinless chicken
    breast fillets, thinly sliced
1 small red pepper, deseeded
    and finely chopped
4 spring onions, trimmed
    and finely chopped
2.5 cm/1 inch piece fresh

root ginger, peeled and
    finely chopped
75 g/3 oz mangetout,
    thinly sliced
75 g/3 oz beansprouts
1 tbsp soy sauce
2 tsp Chinese rice wine or
    dry sherry
2 tsp hoisin or plum sauce

For the wrappers:
3 tbsp plain flour
12–14 spring roll wrappers
300 ml/½ pint vegetable oil
    for deep frying
shredded spring onions,
    to garnish
dipping sauce, to serve

Heat a large wok, add the oil and when hot, add the diced bacon and stir-fry for 2–3 minutes, or until golden. Add the chicken and pepper and stir-fry for a further 2–3 minutes. Add the remaining filling ingredients and stir-fry for 3–4 minutes until all the vegetables are tender. Turn into a colander and leave to drain as the mixture cools completely.

Blend the flour with about 1½ tablespoons of water to form a paste. Soften each wrapper in a plate of warm water for 1–2 seconds, then place on a chopping board. Put 2–3 tablespoons of filling on the near edge. Fold the edge over the filling to cover. Fold in each side and roll up. Seal the edge with a little flour paste and press to seal securely. Transfer to a baking sheet, seam-side down.

Heat the oil in a large wok to 190°C/375°F, or until a small cube of bread browns in about 30 seconds. Working in batches of 3–4, fry the spring rolls until they are crisp and golden, turning once (about 2 minutes). Remove and drain on absorbent kitchen paper. Arrange the spring rolls on a serving plate, garnish with spring onion tassels and serve hot with dipping sauce.

Try This: FOR AN ALTERNATIVE: 320   FOR A DIFFERENT MEAT OPTION: 198

Cantonese Chicken Wings

SERVES 4

3 tbsp hoisin sauce
2 tbsp dark soy sauce
1 tbsp sesame oil
1 garlic clove, peeled
 and crushed
2.5 cm/1 inch piece fresh root

ginger, peeled and grated
1 tbsp Chinese rice wine
 or dry sherry
2 tsp chilli bean sauce
2 tsp red or white
 wine vinegar

2 tbsp soft light brown sugar
900 g/2 lb large chicken wings
50 g/2 oz cashew
 nuts, chopped
2 spring onions, trimmed
 and finely chopped

Preheat the oven to 220°C/425°F/Gas Mark 7, 15 minutes before cooking. Place the hoisin sauce, soy sauce, sesame oil, garlic, ginger, Chinese rice wine or sherry, chilli bean sauce, vinegar and sugar in a small saucepan with 6 tablespoons of water. Bring to the boil, stirring occasionally, then simmer for about 30 seconds. Remove the glaze from the heat.

Place the chicken wings in a roasting tin in a single layer. Pour over the glaze and stir until the wings are coated thoroughly.

Cover the tin loosely with foil, place in the preheated oven and roast for 25 minutes. Remove the foil, baste the wings and cook for a further 5 minutes.

Reduce the oven temperature to 190°C/375°F/Gas Mark 5. Turn the wings over and sprinkle with the chopped cashew nuts and spring onions. Return to the oven and cook for 5 minutes, or until the nuts are lightly browned, the glaze is sticky and the wings are tender. Remove from the oven and leave to stand for 5 minutes before arranging on a warmed platter. Serve immediately with finger bowls and plenty of napkins.

Try This: FOR AN ALTERNATIVE: 296   FOR A DIFFERENT MEAT OPTION: 40

Deep–fried Chicken Wings

SERVES 4

2 tsp turmeric
1 tsp hot chilli powder
1 tsp ground coriander
1 tsp ground cumin
3 garlic cloves, peeled
   and crushed

8 chicken wings
2 tbsp orange marmalade
2 tbsp ginger preserve
   or marmalade
1 tsp salt
3 tbsp rice wine vinegar

2 tbsp tomato ketchup
1 litre/1¾ pints vegetable oil
   for deep frying
lime wedges, to garnish

Blend the turmeric, chilli powder, ground coriander, ground cumin and garlic together in a small bowl. Dry the chicken wings thoroughly, using absorbent kitchen paper, then rub the spice mixture on to the skin of each chicken wing. Cover and chill in the refrigerator for at least 2 hours.

Meanwhile, make the dipping sauce by mixing together the marmalade, ginger preserve, salt, rice wine vinegar and tomato ketchup in a small saucepan. Heat until blended, leave to cool, then serve. If using straight away, spoon into a small dipping bowl, but if using later, pour into a container with a close-fitting lid and store in the refrigerator.

Pour the oil into the wok and heat to 190°C/375°F, or until a small cube of bread dropped in the oil turns golden brown in 30 seconds. Cook 2–3 chicken wings at a time, lowering them into the hot oil, and frying for 3–4 minutes. Remove the wings using a slotted spoon, and drain on absorbent kitchen paper. You may need to reheat the oil before cooking each batch.

When all the chicken wings are cooked, arrange on a warmed serving dish, garnish with the lime wedges and serve.

Try This: FOR AN ALTERNATIVE: 294   FOR A DIFFERENT MEAT OPTION: 176

Orange–roasted Whole Chicken

SERVES 6

1 small orange, thinly sliced
50 g/2 oz sugar
1.4 kg/3 lb oven-ready chicken
1 small bunch fresh coriander
1 small bunch fresh mint
2 tbsp olive oil

1 tsp Chinese five-
   spice powder
½ tsp paprika
1 tsp fennel seeds, crushed
salt and freshly ground
   black pepper

sprigs of fresh coriander,
   to garnish
freshly cooked vegetables,
   to serve

Preheat the oven to 190°C/375°F/Gas Mark 5, 10 minutes before cooking. Place the orange slices in a small saucepan, cover with water, bring to the boil, then simmer for 2 minutes and drain. Place the sugar in a clean saucepan with 150 ml/¼ pint fresh water. Stir over a low heat until the sugar dissolves, then bring to the boil, add the drained orange slices and simmer for 10 minutes. Remove from the heat and leave in the syrup until cold.

Remove any excess fat from inside the chicken. Starting at the neck end, carefully loosen the skin of the chicken over the breast and legs without tearing. Push the orange slices under the loosened skin with the coriander and mint.

Mix together the olive oil, Chinese five-spice powder, paprika and crushed fennel seeds and season to taste with salt and pepper. Brush the chicken skin generously with this mixture. Transfer to a wire rack set over a roasting tin and roast in the preheated oven for 1½ hours, or until the juices run clear when a skewer is inserted into the thickest part of the thigh. Remove from the oven and leave to rest for 10 minutes. Garnish with sprigs of fresh coriander and serve with freshly cooked vegetables.

Try This: FOR AN ALTERNATIVE: 324   FOR A DIFFERENT MEAT OPTION: 184

Grilled Spiced Chicken with Tomato & Shallot Chutney

SERVES 4

3 tbsp sunflower oil
2 hot red chillies, deseeded
    and chopped
3 garlic cloves, peeled
    and chopped
1 tsp ground turmeric
1 tsp cumin seeds
1 tsp fennel seeds
1 tbsp freshly chopped basil
1 tbsp dark brown sugar

125 ml/4 fl oz rice or white
    wine vinegar
2 tsp sesame oil
4 large chicken breast
    quarters, wings attached
225 g/8 oz small shallots,
    peeled and halved
2 tbsp Chinese rice wine
    or dry sherry
50 g/2 oz caster sugar

175 g/6 oz cherry tomatoes,
    halved
2 tbsp light soy sauce

To garnish:
sprigs of fresh coriander
sprigs of fresh dill
lemon wedges

Preheat the grill to medium, 5 minutes before cooking. Heat a wok or large frying pan, add 1 tablespoon of the sunflower oil and when hot, add the chillies, garlic, turmeric, cumin, fennel seeds, and basil. Fry for 5 minutes, add the sugar and 2 tablespoons of vinegar and stir until the sugar has dissolved. Remove, stir in the sesame oil and leave to cool.

Cut 3 or 4 deep slashes in the thickest part of the chicken breasts. Spread the spice paste over the chicken, place in a dish, cover and marinate in the refrigerator for at least 4 hours or overnight.

Heat the remaining sunflower oil in a saucepan, add the shallots and remaining garlic and cook gently for 15 minutes. Add the remaining vinegar, Chinese rice wine or sherry and caster sugar with 50 ml/2 fl oz water. Bring to the boil and simmer rapidly for 10 minutes, or until thickened. Add the tomatoes with the soy sauce. Simmer for 5–10 minutes, or until the liquid is reduced. Leave the chutney to cool.

Transfer the chicken pieces to a grill pan and cook under the preheated grill for 15–20 minutes on each side, or until the chicken is cooked through, basting frequently. Garnish with coriander sprigs and lemon wedges and serve immediately with the chutney.

Try This: FOR AN ALTERNATIVE: 330 FOR A DIFFERENT MEAT OPTION: 208

Lemon Chicken

SERVES 4

450 g/1 lb skinless, boneless chicken breast fillets, cubed
1 medium egg white, beaten
1 tsp salt
1 tbsp sesame oil
1 tbsp cornflour
200 ml/7 fl oz groundnut oil

75 ml/3 fl oz chicken stock
zest and juice of 1 lemon
1 tbsp caster sugar
1 tbsp light soy sauce
2 tbsp Chinese rice wine or dry sherry
3 large garlic cloves, peeled

and finely chopped
1–2 tsp dried red chillies, crushed
shredded fresh red chillies, to garnish
freshly steamed white rice, to serve

Place the cubes of chicken in a large bowl then add the beaten egg white, salt, 1 teaspoon of sesame oil and 1 teaspoon of cornflour. Mix lightly together until all the chicken is coated, then chill in the refrigerator for 20 minutes.

Heat the wok until very hot and add the oil. When hot, remove the wok from the heat and add the chicken. Stir-fry for 2 minutes, or until the chicken turns white, then remove with a slotted spoon and drain on absorbent kitchen paper.

Wipe the wok clean and heat it until hot again. Add the stock, lemon zest and juice, sugar, soy sauce, Chinese rice wine or sherry, garlic and crushed chillies and bring to the boil. Blend the remaining cornflour to a smooth paste with 1 tablespoon of water and add to the wok. Stir, then simmer for 1 minute. Add the chicken cubes and stir-fry for 2–3 minutes. Add the remaining sesame oil, garnish with shredded chillies and serve immediately with freshly steamed rice.

 Try This: FOR AN ALTERNATIVE: 298   FOR A DIFFERENT MEAT OPTION: 234

Chicken in Black Bean Sauce

SERVES 4

450 g/1 lb skinless, boneless chicken breast fillets, cut into strips
1 tbsp light soy sauce
2 tbsp Chinese rice wine or dry sherry
salt
1 tsp caster sugar
1 tsp sesame oil
2 tsp cornflour

2 tbsp sunflower oil
2 green peppers, deseeded and diced
1 tbsp freshly grated root ginger
2 garlic cloves, peeled and roughly chopped
2 shallots, peeled and finely chopped
4 spring onions, trimmed

and finely sliced
3 tbsp salted black beans, chopped
150 ml/¼ pint chicken stock
shredded spring onions, to garnish
freshly cooked egg noodles, to serve

Place the chicken strips in a large bowl. Mix the soy sauce, Chinese rice wine or sherry, a little salt, caster sugar, sesame oil and cornflour with the chicken.

Heat the wok over a high heat, add the oil and when very hot, add the chicken strips and stir-fry for 2 minutes. Add the green peppers and stir-fry for a further 2 minutes. Then add the ginger, garlic, shallots, spring onions and black beans and continue to stir-fry for another 2 minutes.

Add 4 tablespoons of the stock, stir-fry for 1 minute, then pour in the remaining stock and bring to the boil. Reduce the heat and simmer the sauce for 3–4 minutes, or until the chicken is cooked and the sauce has thickened slightly. Garnish with the shredded spring onions and serve immediately with noodles.

Try This: FOR AN ALTERNATIVE: 322   FOR A DIFFERENT MEAT OPTION: 196

Chicken Chow Mein

SERVES 4

225 g/8 oz egg noodles
5 tsp sesame oil
4 tsp light soy sauce
2 tbsp Chinese rice wine
 or dry sherry
salt and freshly ground
 black pepper
225 g/8 oz skinless chicken

breast fillets, cut into strips
3 tbsp groundnut oil
2 garlic cloves, peeled and
 finely chopped
50 g/2 oz mangetout,
 finely sliced
50 g/2 oz cooked ham,
 cut into fine strips

2 tsp dark soy sauce
pinch of sugar

To garnish:
shredded spring onions
toasted sesame seeds

Bring a large saucepan of water to the boil and add the noodles. Cook for 3–5 minutes, drain and plunge into cold water. Drain again, add 1 tablespoon of the sesame oil and stir lightly.

Place 2 teaspoons of light soy sauce, 1 tablespoon of Chinese rice wine or sherry, and 1 teaspoon of the sesame oil, with seasoning to taste, in a bowl. Add the chicken and stir well. Cover lightly and leave to marinate in the refrigerator for about 15 minutes.

Heat the wok over a high heat, add 1 tablespoon of the groundnut oil and when very hot, add the chicken and its marinade and stir-fry for 2 minutes. Remove the chicken and juices and reserve. Wipe the wok clean with absorbent kitchen paper.

Reheat the wok and add the oil. Add the garlic and toss in the oil for 20 seconds. Add the mangetout peas and the ham and stir-fry for 1 minute. Add the noodles, remaining light soy sauce, Chinese rice wine or sherry, the dark soy sauce and sugar. Season to taste with salt and pepper and stir-fry for 2 minutes.

Add the chicken and juices to the wok and stir-fry for 4 minutes, or until the chicken is cooked. Drizzle over the remaining sesame oil. Garnish with spring onions and sesame seeds and serve.

Try This: FOR AN ALTERNATIVE: 322   FOR A DIFFERENT MEAT OPTION: 188

Thai Coconut Chicken

SERVES 4

1 tsp cumin seeds
1 tsp mustard seeds
1 tsp coriander seeds
1 tsp turmeric
1 bird's-eye chilli, deseeded
 and finely chopped
1 tbsp freshly grated
 root ginger

2 garlic cloves, peeled and
 finely chopped
125 ml/4 fl oz double cream
8 skinless chicken thighs
2 tbsp groundnut oil
1 onion, peeled and
 finely sliced
200 ml/7 fl oz coconut milk

salt and freshly ground
 black pepper
4 tbsp freshly chopped
 coriander
2 spring onions, shredded,
 to garnish
freshly cooked Thai fragrant
 rice, to serve

Heat the wok and add the cumin seeds, mustard seeds and coriander seeds. Dry-fry over a low to medium heat for 2 minutes, or until the fragrance becomes stronger and the seeds start to pop. Add the turmeric and leave to cool slightly. Grind the spices in a pestle and mortar or blend to a fine powder in a food processor.

Mix the chilli, ginger, garlic and the cream together in a small bowl, add the ground spices and mix Place the chicken thighs in a shallow dish and spread the spice paste over them.

Heat the wok over a high heat, add the oil and when hot, add the onion and stir-fry until golden brown. Add the chicken and spice paste. Cook for 5–6 minutes, stirring occasionally, until evenly coloured. Add the coconut milk and season to taste with salt and pepper. Simmer the chicken for 15–20 minutes, or until the thighs are cooked through, taking care not to allow the mixture to boil. Stir in the chopped coriander and serve immediately with the freshly cooked rice sprinkled with shredded spring onions.

 Try This: FOR AN ALTERNATIVE: 288   FOR A DIFFERENT MEAT OPTION: 194

Stir–fried Chicken with Basil

SERVES 4

3 tbsp sunflower oil
3 tbsp green curry paste
450 g/1 lb skinless, boneless
   chicken breast fillets,
   trimmed and cut into cubes
8 cherry tomatoes
100 ml/4 fl oz coconut cream

2 tbsp soft brown sugar
2 tbsp Thai fish sauce
1 red chilli, deseeded
   and thinly sliced
1 green chilli, deseeded
   and thinly sliced
75 g/3 oz fresh torn

basil leaves
sprigs of fresh coriander,
   to garnish
freshly steamed white rice,
   to serve

Heat the wok, then add the oil and heat for 1 minute. Add the green curry paste and cook, stirring, for 1 minute to release the flavour and cook the paste. Add the chicken and stir-fry over a high heat for 2 minutes, making sure the chicken is coated thoroughly with the green curry paste.

Reduce the heat under the wok, then add the cherry tomatoes and cook, stirring gently, for 2–3 minutes, or until the tomatoes burst and begin to disintegrate into the green curry paste.

Add half the coconut cream to the wok with the brown sugar, Thai fish sauce and the red and green chillies. Stir-fry gently for 5 minutes, or until the sauce is amalgamated and the chicken is cooked thoroughly.

Just before serving, sprinkle the chicken with the torn basil leaves and add the remaining coconut cream, then serve immediately with freshly steamed white rice garnished with fresh coriander sprigs.

 Try This: FOR AN ALTERNATIVE: 314   FOR A DIFFERENT MEAT OPTION: 56

Chicken & Cashew Nuts

SERVES 4

450 g/1 lb skinless, boneless chicken breast fillets, cut into 1 cm/½ inch cubes
1 medium egg white, beaten
1 tsp salt
1 tsp sesame oil
2 tsp cornflour

300 ml/½ pint groundnut oil for deep frying
2 tsp sunflower oil
50 g/2 oz unsalted cashews
4 spring onions, shredded
50 g/2 oz mangetout, diagonally sliced

1 tbsp Chinese rice wine
1 tbsp light soy sauce
shredded spring onions, to garnish
freshly steamed white rice with fresh coriander leaves, to serve

Place the cubes of chicken in a large bowl. Add the egg white, salt, sesame oil and cornflour. Mix well to ensure the chicken is coated thoroughly. Chill in the refrigerator for 20 minutes.

Heat the wok until very hot, add the groundnut oil and when hot, remove the wok from the heat and add the chicken. Stir continuously to prevent the chicken from sticking to the wok. When the chicken turns white, after about 2 minutes, remove it using a slotted spoon and reserve. Discard the oil.

Wipe the wok clean with absorbent kitchen paper and heat it again until very hot. Add the sunflower oil and heat. When hot, add the cashew nuts, spring onions and mangetout and stir-fry for 1 minute.

Add the rice wine and soy sauce. Return the chicken to the wok and stir-fry for 2 minutes. Garnish with shredded spring onions and serve immediately with freshly steamed rice sprinkled with fresh coriander.

Try This: FOR AN ALTERNATIVE: 314 FOR A DIFFERENT MEAT OPTION: 202

Stir–fried Chicken with Spinach, Tomatoes & Pine Nuts

SERVES 4

50 g/2 oz pine nuts
2 tbsp sunflower oil
1 red onion, peeled and
   finely chopped
450 g/1 lb skinless, boneless
   chicken breast fillets, cut

into strips
450 g/1 lb cherry
   tomatoes, halved
225 g/8 oz baby spinach,
   washed
salt and freshly ground

black pepper
¼ tsp freshly grated nutmeg
2 tbsp balsamic vinegar
50 g/2 oz raisins
freshly cooked ribbon noodles
   tossed in butter, to serve

Heat the wok and add the pine nuts. Dry-fry for about 2 minutes, shaking often to ensure that they toast but do not burn. Remove and reserve. Wipe any dust from the wok.

Heat the wok again, add the oil and when hot, add the red onion and stir-fry for 2 minutes. Add the chicken and stir-fry for 2–3 minutes, or until golden brown. Reduce the heat, toss in the cherry tomatoes and stir-fry gently until the tomatoes start to disintegrate.

Add the baby spinach and stir-fry for 2–3 minutes, or until they start to wilt. Season to taste with salt and pepper, then sprinkle in the grated nutmeg and drizzle in the balsamic vinegar. Finally, stir in the raisins and reserved toasted pine nuts. Serve immediately on a bed of buttered ribbon noodles.

Try This: FOR AN ALTERNATIVE: 312   FOR A DIFFERENT MEAT OPTION: 216

Chicken & Red Pepper Curried Rice

SERVES 4

350 g/12 oz long-grain rice
salt
1 large egg white
1 tbsp cornflour
300 g/11 oz skinless chicken
    breast fillets, cut into chunks

3 tbsp groundnut oil
1 red pepper, deseeded and
    roughly chopped
1 tbsp curry powder or paste
125 ml/4 fl oz chicken stock
1 tsp sugar

1 tbsp Chinese rice wine or
    dry sherry
1 tbsp light soy sauce
sprigs of fresh coriander,
    to garnish

Wash the rice in several changes of water until the water remains relatively clear. Drain well. Put into a saucepan and cover with fresh water. Add a little salt and bring to the boil. Cook for 7–8 minutes until tender. Drain and refresh under cold running water, then drain again and reserve.

Lightly whisk the egg white with 1 teaspoon of salt and 2 teaspoons of cornflour until smooth. Add the chicken and mix together well. Cover and chill in the refrigerator for 20 minutes.

Heat the oil in a wok until moderately hot. Add the chicken mixture to the wok and stir-fry for 2–3 minutes until all the chicken has turned white. Using a slotted spoon, lift the cubes of chicken from the wok, then drain on absorbent kitchen paper.

Add the red peppers to the wok and stir-fry for 1 minute over a high heat. Add the curry powder or paste and cook for a further 30 seconds, then add the chicken stock, sugar, Chinese rice wine and soy sauce. Mix the remaining cornflour with 1 teaspoon of cold water and add to the wok, stirring. Bring to the boil and simmer gently for 1 minute.

Return the chicken to the wok, then simmer for a further 1 minute before adding the rice. Stir over a medium heat for another 2 minutes until heated through. Garnish with the sprigs of coriander and serve.

Try This: FOR AN ALTERNATIVE: 322   FOR A DIFFERENT MEAT OPTION: 232

Chicken & Lamb Satay

MAKES 16

225 g/8 oz skinless, boneless chicken
225 g/8 oz lean lamb

For the marinade:
1 small onion, peeled and finely chopped
2 garlic cloves, peeled and crushed
2.5 cm/1 inch piece fresh root ginger, peeled and grated
4 tbsp soy sauce
1 tsp ground coriander
2 tsp dark brown sugar
2 tbsp lime juice
1 tbsp vegetable oil

For the peanut sauce:
300 ml/½ pint coconut milk
4 tbsp crunchy peanut butter
1 tbsp Thai fish sauce
1 tsp lime juice
1 tbsp chilli powder
1 tbsp brown sugar
salt and freshly ground black pepper

To garnish:
sprigs of fresh coriander
lime wedges

Preheat the grill just before cooking. Soak 16 bamboo skewers for 30 minutes before required. Cut the chicken and lamb into thin strips, about 7.5 cm/3 inches long and place in 2 shallow dishes. Blend all the marinade ingredients together, then pour half over the chicken and half over the lamb. Stir until lightly coated, then cover with clingfilm and leave to marinate in the refrigerator for at least 2 hours, turning occasionally.

Remove the chicken and lamb from the marinade and thread on to the skewers. Reserve the marinade. Cook under the preheated grill for 8–10 minutes or until cooked, turning and brushing with the marinade.

0Meanwhile, make the peanut sauce. Blend the coconut milk with the peanut butter, fish sauce, lime juice, chilli powder and sugar. Pour into a saucepan and cook gently for 5 minutes, stirring occasionally, then season to taste with salt and pepper. Garnish with coriander sprigs and lime wedges and serve the satays with the prepared sauce.

Try This: FOR AN ALTERNATIVE: 292   FOR A DIFFERENT MEAT OPTION: 220

Chicken Wraps

SERVES 4

For the stir-fried chicken:
4 skinless chicken breast
    fillets
juice and finely grated zest
    of 1 lime
1 tbsp caster sugar
2 tsp dried oregano
½ tsp ground cinnamon
¼ tsp cayenne pepper

3 tbsp sunflower oil
2 onions, peeled and sliced
1 green, 1 red and 1 yellow
    pepper, deseeded and
    sliced
salt and freshly ground
    black pepper

For the tortillas:
250 g/9 oz plain flour
pinch of salt
¼ tsp baking powder
50 g/2 oz white vegetable fat

To serve:
soured cream
guacamole

Slice the chicken across the grain into 2 cm/¾ inch wide strips. Place in a bowl with the lime zest and juice, sugar, oregano, cinnamon and cayenne pepper. Mix well and leave to marinate while making the tortillas.

Sift the flour, salt and baking powder into a bowl. Rub in the white fat, then sprinkle over 4 tablespoons of warm water and mix to a stiff dough. Knead on a lightly floured surface for 10 minutes until smooth and elastic. Divide the dough into 12 equal pieces and roll out each to a 15 cm/6 inch circle. Cover with clingfilm to prevent them drying out before you cook them. Heat a non-stick wok and cook each tortilla for about 1 minute on each side, or until golden and slightly blistered. Remove the tortillas and keep them warm and pliable in a clean tea towel.

Heat 2 tablespoons of the oil in the wok and stir-fry the onions for 5 minutes until lightly coloured. Remove with a slotted spoon and reserve. Add the remaining oil to the wok and heat. Drain the chicken from the marinade and add it to the wok. Stir-fry for 5 minutes, then return the onions, add the pepper slices and cook for a further 3–4 minutes, or until the chicken is cooked through and the vegetables are tender. Season to taste with salt and pepper and serve immediately with the tortillas, soured cream and guacamole.

Try This: FOR AN ALTERNATIVE: 232   FOR A DIFFERENT MEAT OPTION: 206

Sweet & Sour Rice with Chicken

SERVES 4

4 spring onions
2 tsp sesame oil
1 tsp Chinese five-spice
  powder
450 g/1 lb chicken breast,
  cut into cubes
1 tbsp oil

1 garlic clove, peeled
  and crushed
1 medium onion, peeled and
  sliced into thin wedges
225 g/8 oz long-grain
  white rice
600 ml/1 pint water

4 tbsp tomato ketchup
1 tbsp tomato purée
2 tbsp honey
1 tbsp vinegar
1 tbsp dark soy sauce
1 carrot, peeled and cut
  into matchsticks

Trim the spring onions, then cut lengthways into fine strips. Drop into a large bowl of iced water and reserve.

Mix together the sesame oil and Chinese five-spice powder and use to rub into the cubed chicken. Heat the wok, then add the oil and when hot, cook the garlic and onion for 2–3 minutes, or until transparent and softened.

Add the chicken and stir-fry over a medium-high heat until the chicken is golden and cooked through. Using a slotted spoon, remove from the wok and keep warm.

Stir the rice into the wok and add the water, tomato ketchup, tomato purée, honey, vinegar and soy sauce. Stir well to mix. Bring to the boil, then simmer until almost all of the liquid is absorbed. Stir in the carrot and reserved chicken and continue to cook for 3–4 minutes.

Drain the spring onions, which will have become curly, and use to garnish the rice and chicken. Serve immediately.

Try This: FOR AN ALTERNATIVE: 326   FOR A DIFFERENT MEAT OPTION: 218

Herbed Hasselback Potatoes with Roast Chicken

SERVES 4

8 medium, evenly-sized potatoes, peeled
3 large sprigs of fresh rosemary
1 tbsp olive oil (not extra-virgin)

salt and freshly ground black pepper
350 g/12 oz baby parsnips, peeled
350 g/12 oz baby carrots, peeled

350 g/12 oz baby leeks, trimmed
75 g/3 oz butter
finely grated rind of 1 lemon, preferably unwaxed
1.6 kg/3½ lb whole chicken

Preheat the oven to 200°C/400°F/Gas Mark 6, about 15 minutes before cooking. Place a chopstick on either side of a potato and, with a sharp knife, cut down through the potato until you reach the chopsticks; take care not to cut right through the potato. Repeat these cuts every 5 mm/¼ inch along the length of the potato. Carefully ease 2–4 of the slices apart and slip in a few rosemary sprigs. Repeat with remaining potatoes. Brush with the oil and season well with salt and pepper.

Place the seasoned potatoes in a large roasting tin. Add the parsnips, carrots and leeks to the potatoes in the tin, cover with a wire rack or trivet.

Beat the butter and lemon rind together and season to taste. Smear the chicken with the lemon butter and place on the rack over the vegetables.

Roast in the preheated oven for 1 hour 40 minutes, basting the chicken and vegetables occasionally, until cooked thoroughly. The juices should run clear when the thigh is pierced with a skewer. Place the cooked chicken on a warmed serving platter, arrange the roast vegetables around it and serve immediately.

Try This: FOR AN ALTERNATIVE: 298   FOR A DIFFERENT MEAT OPTION: 244

Chicken with Roasted Fennel & Citrus Rice

SERVES 4

2 tsp fennel seeds
1 tbsp freshly
    chopped oregano
1 garlic clove, peeled
    and crushed
salt and freshly ground
    black pepper
4 chicken quarters,
    about 175 g/6 oz each

½ lemon, finely sliced
1 fennel bulb, trimmed
2 tsp olive oil
4 plum tomatoes
25 g/1 oz stoned green olives

To garnish:
fennel fronds
orange slices

Citrus rice:
225 g/8 oz long-grain rice
juice and finely grated rind
    of ½ lemon
150 ml/¼ pint orange juice
450 ml/¾ pint boiling chicken
    or vegetable stock

Preheat the oven to 200°C/400°F/Gas Mark 6. Lightly crush the fennel seeds and mix with oregano, garlic, salt and pepper. Place between the skin and flesh of the chicken breasts, careful not to tear the skin. Arrange the lemon slices on top of the chicken.

Cut the fennel into 8 wedges. Place on baking tray with the chicken. Lightly brush the fennel with the oil. Cook the chicken and fennel on the top shelf of the preheated oven for 10 minutes.

Meanwhile, put the rice in a 2.3 litre/4 pint ovenproof dish. Stir in the lemon rind and juice, orange juice and stock. Cover with a lid and put on the middle shelf of the oven.

Reduce the oven temperature to 180°C/350°F/Gas Mark 4. Cook the chicken for a further 40 minutes, turning the fennel wedges and lemon slices once. Deseed and chop the tomatoes. Add to the tray and cook for 5–10 minutes. Remove from the oven.

When cooled slightly, remove the chicken skin and discard. Fluff the rice, scatter olives over the dish. Garnish with fennel fronds, orange slices and serve.

Try This: FOR AN ALTERNATIVE: 340 FOR A DIFFERENT MEAT OPTION: 234

Braised Chicken in Beer

SERVES 4

4 chicken joints, skinned
125 g/4 oz pitted dried prunes
2 bay leaves
12 shallots
2 tsp olive oil
125 g/4 oz small button
    mushrooms, wiped
1 tsp soft dark brown sugar

½ tsp wholegrain mustard
2 tsp tomato purée
150 ml/¼ pint light ale
150 ml/¼ pint chicken stock
salt and freshly ground
    black pepper
2 tsp cornflour
2 tsp lemon juice

2 tbsp fresh parsley,
    chopped
flat-leaf parsley, to garnish

To serve:
mashed potatoes
seasonal green vegetables

Preheat the oven to 170°C/325°F/Gas Mark 3. Cut each chicken joint in half and put in an ovenproof casserole with the prunes and bay leaves.

To peel the shallots, put in a small bowl and cover with boiling water. Drain them after 2 minutes and rinse under cold water until cool enough to handle. The skins should then peel away easily.

Heat the oil in a large non-stick frying pan. Add the shallots and gently cook for about 5 minutes until beginning to colour. Add the mushrooms to the pan and cook for a further 3–4 minutes until both the mushrooms and onions are softened. Sprinkle the sugar over the shallots and mushrooms, then add the mustard, tomato purée, ale and chicken stock. Season to taste with salt and pepper and bring to the boil, stirring to combine. Carefully pour over the chicken.

Cover the casserole and cook in the preheated oven for 1 hour. Blend the cornflour with the lemon juice and 1 tablespoon of cold water and stir into the chicken casserole. Return the casserole to the oven for a further 10 minutes or until the chicken is cooked and the vegetables are tender.

Remove the bay leaves and stir in the chopped parsley. Garnish the chicken with the flat-leaf parsley. Serve with the mashed potatoes and fresh green vegetables.

 Try This: FOR AN ALTERNATIVE: 342   FOR A DIFFERENT MEAT OPTION: 174

Spicy Chicken Skewers with Mango Tabbouleh

SERVES 4

400 g/14 oz chicken breast fillet
200 ml/7 fl oz natural yoghurt
1 garlic clove, peeled and crushed
1 small red chilli, deseeded and finely chopped
½ tsp ground turmeric

juice and finely grated rind of ½ lemon
sprigs of fresh mint, to garnish

Mango tabbouleh:
175 g/6 oz bulgur wheat
1 tsp olive oil
juice of ½ lemon

½ red onion, finely chopped
1 ripe mango, halved, stoned, peeled and chopped
¼ cucumber, finely diced
2 tbsp freshly chopped parsley
2 tbsp freshly shredded mint
salt and finely ground black pepper

If using wooden skewers, presoak them in cold water for at least 30 minutes. (This stops them from burning during grilling.) Cut the chicken into 5 x 1 cm/2 x ½ inch strips and place in a shallow dish.

Mix together the yoghurt, garlic, chilli, turmeric, lemon rind and juice. Pour over the chicken and toss to coat. Cover and leave to marinate in the refrigerator for up to 8 hours.

To make the tabbouleh, put the bulgur wheat in a bowl. Pour over enough boiling water to cover. Put a plate over the bowl. Leave to soak for 20 minutes. Whisk together the oil and lemon juice in a bowl. Add the red onion and leave to marinate for 10 minutes.

Drain the bulgur wheat and squeeze out any excess moisture in a clean tea towel. Add to the red onion with the mango, cucumber and herbs and season to taste with salt and pepper. Toss together. Thread the chicken strips on to 8 wooden or metal skewers. Cook under a hot grill for 8 minutes. Turn and brush with the marinade until the chicken is lightly browned and cooked through. Spoon the tabbouleh on to individual plates. Arrange the chicken skewers on top and garnish with the sprigs of mint. Serve warm or cold.

Try This: FOR AN ALTERNATIVE: 326   FOR A DIFFERENT MEAT OPTION: 208

Sauvignon Chicken & Mushroom Filo Pie

SERVES 4

1 onion, peeled and chopped
1 leek, trimmed and chopped
225 ml/8 fl oz chicken stock
3 x 175 g/6 oz chicken breasts
150 ml/¼ pint dry
    white wine
1 bay leaf
175 g/6 oz baby

button mushrooms
2 tbsp plain flour
1 tbsp freshly
    chopped tarragon
salt and freshly ground
    black pepper
sprig of fresh parsley,
    to garnish

seasonal vegetables,
    to serve

For the topping:
75 g/3 oz (about 5 sheets)
    filo pastry
1 tbsp sunflower oil
1 tsp sesame seeds

Preheat the oven to 190°C/375°F/Gas Mark 5. Put the onion and leek in a heavy-based saucepan with 125 ml/4 fl oz of the stock. Bring to the boil, cover and simmer for 5 minutes, then uncover and cook until all the stock has evaporated and the vegetables are tender.

Cut the chicken into bite-sized cubes. Add to the pan with the remaining stock, wine and bay leaf. Cover and gently simmer for 5 minutes. Add the mushrooms and simmer for a further 5 minutes.

Blend the flour with 3 tablespoons of cold water. Stir into the pan and cook, stirring all the time until the sauce has thickened. Stir the tarragon into the sauce and season with salt and pepper. Spoon the mixture into a 1.2 litre/2 pint pie dish, discarding the bay leaf.

Lightly brush a sheet of filo pastry with a little of the oil. Crumple the pastry slightly. Arrange on top of the filling. Repeat with the remaining filo sheets and oil, then sprinkle the top of the pie with the sesame seeds.

Bake the pie on the middle shelf of the preheated oven for 20 minutes until the filo pastry topping is golden and crisp. Garnish with a sprig of parsley. Serve the pie immediately with the seasonal vegetables.

Try This: FOR AN ALTERNATIVE: 286   FOR A DIFFERENT MEAT OPTION: 228

Chilli Roast Chicken

SERVES 4

3 medium-hot fresh red
   chillies, deseeded
½ tsp ground turmeric
1 tsp cumin seeds
1 tsp coriander seeds
2 garlic cloves, peeled
   and crushed
2.5 cm/1 inch piece fresh root
   ginger, peeled and chopped

1 tbsp lemon juice
1 tbsp olive oil
2 tbsp roughly chopped
   fresh coriander
½ tsp salt
freshly ground black pepper
1.4 kg/3 lb oven-ready chicken
15 g/½ oz unsalted
   butter, melted

550 g/1¼ lb butternut squash
fresh parsley and coriander
   sprigs, to garnish

To serve:
4 baked potatoes
seasonal green vegetables

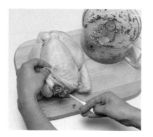

Preheat the oven to 190°C/375°F/Gas Mark 5. Roughly chop the chillies and put in a food processor with the turmeric, cumin seeds, coriander seeds, garlic, ginger, lemon juice, olive oil, coriander, salt, pepper and 2 tablespoons of cold water. Blend to a paste, leaving the ingredients still slightly chunky.

Starting at the neck end of the chicken, gently ease up the skin to loosen it from the breast. Reserve 3 tablespoons of the paste. Push the remaining paste over the chicken breast under the skin, spreading it evenly.

Put the chicken in a large roasting tin. Mix the reserved chilli paste with the melted butter. Brush 1 tablespoon of the paste evenly over the chicken, roast in the preheated oven for 20 minutes.

Meanwhile, halve, peel and scoop out the seeds from the butternut squash. Cut into large chunks and mix in the remaining chilli paste and butter mixture.

Arrange the butternut squash around the chicken. Roast for a further hour, basting with the cooking juices about every 20 minutes until the chicken is fully cooked and the squash tender. Garnish with parsley and coriander. Serve hot with baked potatoes and green vegetables.

Try This: FOR AN ALTERNATIVE: 340   FOR A DIFFERENT MEAT OPTION: 222

Cheesy Chicken Burgers

SERVES 6

1 tbsp sunflower oil
1 small onion, peeled
  and finely chopped
1 garlic clove, peeled
  and crushed
½ red pepper, deseeded and
  finely chopped
450 g/1 lb fresh chicken mince
2 tbsp 0%-fat Greek yoghurt
50 g/2 oz fresh
  brown breadcrumbs

1 tbsp freshly chopped herbs,
  such as parsley or tarragon
50 g/2 oz Cheshire
  cheese, crumbled
salt and freshly ground
  black pepper

**For the sweetcorn and
  carrot relish:**
200 g can sweetcorn, drained
1 carrot, peeled, grated

½ green chilli, deseeded
  and finely chopped
2 tsp cider vinegar
2 tsp light soft brown sugar

To serve:
wholemeal or granary rolls
lettuce
sliced tomatoes
mixed salad leaves

Preheat the grill. Heat the oil in a frying pan and gently cook the onion and garlic for 5 minutes. Add the red pepper and cook for 5 minutes. Transfer into a mixing bowl and reserve.

Add the chicken, yoghurt, breadcrumbs, herbs and cheese and season to taste with salt and pepper. Mix well. Divide the mixture equally into 6 and shape into burgers. Cover and chill in the refrigerator for at least 20 minutes.

To make the relish, put all the ingredients in a small saucepan with 1 tablespoon of water and heat gently, stirring occasionally, until all the sugar has dissolved. Cover and cook over a low heat for 2 minutes, then uncover and cook for a further minute, or until the relish is thick.

Place the burgers on a lightly oiled grill pan and grill under a medium heat for 8–10 minutes on each side, or until browned and completely cooked through.

Warm the rolls if liked, then split in half and fill with the burgers, lettuce, sliced tomatoes and the prepared relish. Serve immediately with the salad leaves.

Try This: FOR AN ALTERNATIVE: 292 FOR A DIFFERENT MEAT OPTION: 352

Chicken Cacciatore

SERVES 4

2–3 tbsp olive oil
125 g/4 oz pancetta or
   streaky bacon, diced
25 g/1 oz plain flour
salt and freshly ground
   black pepper
1.4–1.6 kg/3–3½ lb chicken,
   cut into 8 pieces

2 garlic cloves, peeled
   and chopped
125 ml/4 fl oz red wine
400 g can chopped tomatoes
150 ml/¼ pint chicken stock
12 small onions, peeled
1 bay leaf
1 tsp brown sugar

1 tsp dried oregano
1 green pepper, deseeded
   and chopped
225 g/8 oz chestnut or field
   mushrooms, thickly sliced
2 tbsp freshly chopped parsley
freshly cooked tagliatelle,
   to serve

Heat 1 tablespoon of the olive oil in a large, deep frying pan and add the diced pancetta or bacon and stir-fry for 2–3 minutes, or until crisp and golden brown. Using a slotted spoon, transfer the pancetta or bacon to a plate and reserve.

Season the flour with salt and pepper, then use to coat the chicken. Heat the remaining oil in the pan and brown the chicken pieces on all sides for about 15 minutes. Remove from the pan and add to the bacon.

Stir the garlic into the pan and cook for about 30 seconds. Add the red wine and cook, stirring and scraping any browned bits from the base of the pan. Allow the wine to boil until it is reduced by half. Add the tomatoes, stock, onions, bay leaf, brown sugar and oregano and stir well. Season to taste.

Return the chicken and bacon to the pan and bring to the boil. Cover and simmer for 30 minutes, then stir in the peppers and mushrooms and simmer for a further 15–20 minutes, or until the chicken and vegetables are tender and the sauce is reduced and slightly thickened. Stir in the chopped parsley and serve immediately with freshly cooked tagliatelle.

Try This: FOR AN ALTERNATIVE: 326   FOR A DIFFERENT MEAT OPTION: 252

Mexican Chicken

SERVES 4

1.4 kg/3 lb oven-ready
   chicken, jointed
3 tbsp plain flour
½ tsp ground paprika pepper
salt and freshly ground
   black pepper
2 tsp sunflower oil
1 small onion, peeled
   and chopped
1 red chilli, deseeded and

finely chopped
½ tsp ground cumin
½ tsp dried oregano
300 ml/½ pint chicken or
   vegetable stock
1 green pepper, deseeded
   and sliced
2 tsp cocoa powder
1 tbsp lime juice
2 tsp clear honey

3 tbsp 0%-fat Greek yoghurt

To garnish:
sliced limes
red chilli slices
sprig of fresh oregano

To serve:
freshly cooked rice
fresh green salad leaves

Using a knife, remove the skin from the chicken joints.

In a shallow dish, mix together the flour, paprika, salt and pepper. Coat the chicken on both sides with flour and shake off any excess if necessary. Heat the oil in a large non-stick frying pan. Add the chicken and brown on both sides. Transfer to a plate and reserve.

Add the onion and red chilli to the pan and gently cook for 5 minutes, or until the onion is soft. Stir occasionally. Stir in the cumin and oregano and cook for a further minute. Pour in the stock and bring to the boil. Return the chicken to the pan, cover and cook for 40 minutes. Add the green pepper and cook for 10 minutes, until the chicken is cooked. Remove the chicken and pepper with a slotted spoon and keep warm in a serving dish.

Blend the cocoa powder with 1 tablespoon of warm water. Stir into the sauce, then boil rapidly until the sauce has thickened and reduced by about one third. Stir in the lime juice, honey and yoghurt. Pour the sauce over the chicken and pepper and garnish with the lime slices, chilli and oregano. Serve immediately with the freshly cooked rice and green salad.

Try This: FOR AN ALTERNATIVE: 316   FOR A DIFFERENT MEAT OPTION: 246

Chicken Marengo

SERVES 4

2 tbsp plain flour
salt and freshly ground
   black pepper
4 boneless and skinless
   chicken breasts, cut
   into bite-sized pieces
4 tbsp olive oil

1 Spanish onion, peeled
   and chopped
1 garlic clove, peeled
   and chopped
400 g can chopped tomatoes
2 tbsp sun-dried tomato paste
3 tbsp freshly chopped basil

3 tbsp freshly chopped thyme
125 ml/4 fl oz dry white wine
   or chicken stock
350 g/12 oz rigatoni
3 tbsp freshly chopped
   flat-leaf parsley

Season the flour with salt and pepper and toss the chicken in the flour to coat. Heat 2 tablespoons of the olive oil in a large frying pan and cook the chicken for 7 minutes, or until browned all over, turning occasionally. Remove from the pan using a slotted spoon and keep warm.

Add the remaining oil to the pan, add the onion and cook, stirring occasionally, for 5 minutes, or until softened and starting to brown. Add the garlic, tomatoes, tomato paste, basil and thyme. Pour in the wine or chicken stock and season well. Bring to the boil. Stir in the chicken pieces and simmer for 15 minutes, or until the chicken is tender and the sauce has thickened.

Meanwhile, bring a large pan of lightly salted water to a rolling boil. Add the rigatoni and cook according to the packet instructions, or until 'al dente'.

Drain the rigatoni thoroughly, return to the pan and stir in the chopped parsley. Tip the pasta into a large warmed serving dish or spoon on to individual plates. Spoon over the chicken sauce and serve immediately.

Try This: FOR AN ALTERNATIVE: 310   FOR A DIFFERENT MEAT OPTION: 268

Seared Duck with Pickled Plums

SERVES 4

4 small skinless, boneless
  duck breasts
2 garlic cloves, peeled
  and crushed
1 tsp hot chilli sauce
2 tsp clear honey
2 tsp dark brown sugar
juice of 1 lime

1 tbsp dark soy sauce
6 large plums, halved and
  stones removed
50 g/2 oz caster sugar
50 ml/2 fl oz white
  wine vinegar
¼ tsp dried chilli flakes
¼ tsp ground cinnamon

1 tbsp sunflower oil
150 ml/¼ pint chicken stock
2 tbsp oyster sauce
sprigs of fresh flat-leaf
  parsley, to garnish
freshly cooked noodles,
  to serve

Cut a few deep slashes in each duck breast and place in a shallow dish. Mix together the garlic, chilli sauce, honey, brown sugar, lime juice and soy sauce. Spread over the duck and leave to marinate in the refrigerator for 4 hours or overnight, if time permits, turning occasionally.

Place the plums in a saucepan with the caster sugar, white wine vinegar, chilli flakes and cinnamon and bring to the boil. Simmer gently for 5 minutes, or until the plums have just softened, then leave to cool.

Remove the duck from the marinade and pat dry with absorbent kitchen paper. Reserve the marinade. Heat a wok or large frying pan, add the oil and when hot, brown the duck on both sides. Pour in the stock, oyster sauce and reserved marinade and simmer for 5 minutes. Remove the duck and keep warm.

Remove the plums from their liquid and reserve. Pour the liquid into the duck sauce, bring to the boil, then simmer, uncovered, for 5 minutes, or until reduced and thickened. Arrange the duck on warmed plates. Divide the plums between the plates and spoon over the sauce. Garnish with parsley and serve immediately with noodles.

Try This: FOR AN ALTERNATIVE: 348   FOR A DIFFERENT MEAT OPTION: 274

Crispy Aromatic Duck

SERVES 4–6

2 tbsp Chinese five-spice powder
75 g/3 oz Szechuan peppercorns, lightly crushed
25 g/1 oz whole black peppercorns, lightly crushed
3 tbsp cumin seeds, lightly crushed
200 g/7 oz rock salt
2.7 kg/6 lb oven-ready duck
7.5 cm/3 inch piece fresh root ginger, peeled and cut into 6 slices
6 spring onions, trimmed and cut into 7.5 cm/ 3 inch lengths
cornflour for dusting
1.1 litres/2 pints groundnut oil

To serve:
warm Chinese pancakes
spring onion, cut into shreds
cucumber, cut into slices lengthways
hoisin sauce

Mix together the Chinese five-spice powder, Szechuan and black peppercorns, cumin seeds and salt. Rub the duck inside and out with the spice mixture. Wrap the duck with clingfilm and place in the refrigerator for 24 hours. Brush any loose spices from the duck. Place the ginger and spring onions into the duck cavity and put the duck on a heatproof plate.

Place a wire rack in a wok and pour in boiling water to a depth of 5 cm/2 inches. Lower the duck and plate on to the rack and cover. Steam gently for 2 hours or until the duck is cooked through, pouring off excess fat from time to time and adding more water if necessary. Remove the duck, pour off all the liquid and discard the ginger and spring onions. Leave the duck in a cool place for 2 hours, or until it has dried and cooled.

Cut the duck into quarters and dust lightly with cornflour. Heat the oil in a wok or deep-fat fryer to 190°C/375°F, then deep-fry the duck quarters 2 at a time. Cook the breast for 8–10 minutes and the thighs and legs for 12–14 minutes, or until each piece is heated through. Drain on absorbent kitchen paper, then shred some of it with a fork, ready to be put into pancakes. Serve immediately with warm Chinese pancakes, spring onion shreds, cucumber slices and hoisin sauce.

Try This: FOR AN ALTERNATIVE: 352 FOR A DIFFERENT MEAT OPTION: 208

Duck with Berry Sauce

SERVES 4

4 x 175 g/6 oz boneless
duck breasts
salt and freshly ground
black pepper
1 tsp sunflower oil

For the sauce:
juice of 1 orange

1 bay leaf
3 tbsp redcurrant jelly
150 g/5 oz fresh or frozen
mixed berries
2 tbsp dried cranberries
or cherries
½ tsp soft light brown sugar
1 tbsp balsamic vinegar

1 tsp freshly chopped mint
sprigs of fresh mint, to
garnish

To serve:
freshly cooked potatoes
freshly cooked green beans

Remove the skins from the duck breasts and season with a little salt and pepper. Brush a griddle pan with the oil, then heat on the stove until smoking hot.

Place the duck skinned-side down in the pan. Cook over a medium-high heat for 5 minutes, or until well browned. Turn the duck and cook for 2 minutes. Lower the heat and cook for a further 5–8 minutes, or until cooked but still slightly pink in the centre. Remove from the pan and keep warm.

While the duck is cooking, make the sauce. Put the orange juice, bay leaf, redcurrant jelly, fresh or frozen and dried berries and sugar in a small pan. Add any juices left in the griddle pan to the small pan. Slowly bring to the boil, lower the heat and simmer uncovered for 4–5 minutes, or until the fruit is soft.

Remove the bay leaf. Stir in the vinegar and chopped mint and season to taste with salt and pepper.

Slice the duck breasts on the diagonal and arrange on serving plates. Spoon over the berry sauce and garnish with sprigs of fresh mint. Serve immediately with the potatoes and green beans.

Try This: FOR AN ALTERNATIVE: 344 FOR A DIFFERENT MEAT OPTION: 272

Fried Ginger Rice with Soy Glazed Duck

SERVES 4–6

2 duck breasts, skinned and diagonally cut into thin slices
2–3 tbsp Japanese soy sauce
1 tbsp mirin (sweet rice wine) or sherry
2 tbsp brown sugar
5 cm/2 inch piece of fresh root ginger, peeled and finely chopped

4 tbsp peanut or vegetable oil
2 garlic cloves, peeled and crushed
300 g/11 oz long-grain brown rice
900 ml/1½ pints chicken stock
freshly ground black pepper
125 g/4 oz lean ham, diced
175 g/6 oz mangetout, cut in half diagonally

8 spring onions, trimmed and thinly sliced diagonally
1 tbsp freshly chopped coriander
sweet or hot chilli sauce, to taste (optional)
sprigs of fresh coriander, to garnish

Put the duck slices in a bowl with 1 tablespoon of the soy sauce, the mirin, 1 teaspoon of the sugar and one third of the ginger; stir. Leave to stand.

Heat 2 tablespoons of the oil in a large heavy-based saucepan. Add the garlic and half the remaining ginger and stir-fry for 1 minute. Add the rice and cook for 3 minutes, stirring constantly, until translucent. Stir in all but 125 ml/4 fl oz of the stock, with 1 teaspoon of the soy sauce, and bring to the boil. Season with pepper. Reduce the heat to very low and simmer, covered, for 25–30 minutes until the rice is tender and the liquid is absorbed. Cover and leave to stand.

Heat the remaining oil in a large frying pan or wok. Drain the duck strips and add to the frying pan. Stir-fry for 2–3 minutes until just coloured. Add 1 tablespoon of soy sauce and the remaining sugar and cook for 1 minute until glazed. Transfer to a plate and keep warm.

Stir in the ham, mangetout, spring onions, the remaining ginger and the chopped coriander. Add the remaining stock and duck marinade and cook until the liquid is almost reduced. Fork in the rice and a little chilli sauce to taste (if using); stir well. Turn into a serving dish and top with the duck. Garnish with coriander sprigs and serve immediately.

Try This: FOR AN ALTERNATIVE: 354 FOR A DIFFERENT MEAT OPTION: 212

Aromatic Duck Burgers on Potato Pancakes

SERVES 4

700 g/1½ lb boneless duck breasts
2 tbsp hoisin sauce
1 garlic clove, peeled and finely chopped
4 spring onions, trimmed and finely chopped
2 tbsp Japanese soy sauce

½ tsp Chinese five-spice powder
salt and freshly ground black pepper
freshly chopped coriander, to garnish
extra hoisin sauce, to serve

For the potato pancakes:
450 g/1 lb floury potatoes
1 small onion, peeled and grated
1 small egg, beaten
1 heaped tbsp plain flour

Peel off the thick layer of fat from the duck breasts and cut into small pieces. Put the fat in a small dry saucepan and set over a low heat for 10–15 minutes, or until the fat runs clear and the crackling goes crisp; reserve. Cut the duck meat into pieces and blend in a food processor until coarsely chopped. Spoon into a bowl and add the hoisin sauce, garlic, half the spring onions, soy sauce and Chinese five-spice powder. Season to taste with salt and pepper and shape into 4 burgers. Cover and chill in the refrigerator for 1 hour.

To make the potato pancakes, grate the potatoes into a large bowl, squeeze out the water with your hands, then put on a clean tea towel and twist the ends to squeeze out any remaining water. Return the potato to the bowl, add the onion and egg and mix well. Add the flour, salt and pepper. Stir to blend. Heat about 2 tablespoons of the clear duck fat in a large frying pan. Spoon the potato mixture into 2–4 pattie shapes and cook for 6 minutes, or until golden and crisp, turning once. Keep warm in the oven. Repeat with the remaining mixture, adding duck fat as needed. Preheat the grill and line the grill rack with foil. Brush the burgers with a little of the duck fat and grill for 6–8 minutes, or longer if wished, turning once. Arrange 1–2 potato pancakes on a plate and top with a burger. Spoon over a little hoisin sauce and garnish with the remaining spring onions and coriander.

Try This: FOR AN ALTERNATIVE: 346 FOR A DIFFERENT MEAT OPTION: 242

Brown Rice & Lentil Salad with Duck

SERVES 6

225 g/8 oz Puy lentils, rinsed
4 tbsp olive oil
1 medium onion, peeled and
  finely chopped
200 g/7 oz long-grain
  brown rice
½ tsp dried thyme
450 ml/¾ pint chicken stock
salt and freshly ground
  black pepper
350 g/12 oz shiitake or
  portabella mushrooms,
  trimmed and sliced

375 g/13 oz cooked Chinese-
  style spicy duck or roasted
  duck, sliced into chunks
2 garlic cloves, peeled and
  finely chopped
125 g/4 oz cooked smoked
  ham, diced
2 small courgettes, trimmed,
  diced and blanched
6 spring onions, trimmed
  and thinly sliced
2 tbsp freshly chopped parsley
2 tbsp walnut halves,

toasted and chopped

For the dressing:
2 tbsp red or white
  wine vinegar
1 tbsp balsamic vinegar
1 tsp Dijon mustard
1 tsp clear honey
75 ml/3 fl oz extra-virgin
  olive oil
2–3 tbsp walnut oil

Bring a large saucepan of water to the boil, sprinkle in the lentils, return to the boil, then simmer over a low heat for 30 minutes, or until tender; do not overcook. Drain and rinse under cold running water, then drain again and reserve.

Heat 2 tablespoons of the oil in a saucepan. Add the onion and cook for 2 minutes or until it begins to soften. Stir in the rice with the thyme and stock. Season to taste with salt and pepper and bring to the boil. Cover and simmer for 40 minutes, or until tender and the liquid is absorbed.

Heat the remaining oil in a large frying pan and add the mushrooms. Cook for 5 minutes until golden. Stir in the duck and garlic and cook for 2–3 minutes to heat through. Season well.

To make the dressing, whisk the vinegars, mustard and honey in a large serving bowl, then gradually whisk in the oils. Add the lentils and the rice, then stir lightly together. Gently stir in the ham, blanched courgettes, spring onions and parsley. Season to taste and sprinkle with the walnuts. Serve topped with the duck and mushrooms.

Try This: FOR AN ALTERNATIVE: 350   FOR A DIFFERENT MEAT OPTION: 240

Duck Lasagna with Porcini & Basil

SERVES 6

1.4–1.8 kg/3–4 lb
   duck, quartered
1 onion, unpeeled
   and quartered
2 carrots, peeled and
   cut into pieces
1 celery stalk, cut into pieces
1 leek, trimmed and cut

into pieces
2 garlic cloves, unpeeled
   and smashed
1 tbsp black peppercorns
2 bay leaves
6–8 sprigs of fresh thyme
50 g/2 oz dried porcini
125 ml/4 oz dry sherry

75 g/3 oz butter, diced
1 bunch of fresh basil leaves,
   stripped from stems
24 precooked lasagna sheets
75 g/3 oz Parmesan
   cheese, grated
sprig of parsley, to garnish
mixed salad, to serve

Preheat the oven to 180°C/350°F/Gas Mark 4, 10 minutes before cooking. Put the duck with the vegetables, garlic, peppercorns, bay leaves and thyme into a large stock pot and cover with cold water. Bring to the boil, skimming off any fat, then reduce the heat and simmer for 1 hour. Transfer the duck to a bowl and cool slightly.

When cool enough to handle, remove the meat from the duck and dice. Return all the bones and trimmings to the simmering stock and continue to simmer for 1 hour. Strain the stock into a large bowl and leave until cold. Remove and discard the fat that has risen to the top of the stock.

Put the porcini in a colander and rinse under cold running water. Leave for 1 minute to dry off, then turn out on to a chopping board and chop finely. Place in a small bowl, then pour over the sherry and leave for about 1 hour, or until the porcini are plump and all the sherry is absorbed. Heat 25 g/1 oz of the butter in a frying pan. Shred the basil leaves and add to the hot butter, stirring until wilted. Add the soaked porcini and any liquid, mix well and reserve. Oil a 30.5 x 23 cm/12 x 9 inch deep baking dish and pour a little stock into the base. Cover with 6–8 lasagna sheets, making sure they overlap slightly . Continue to layer the pasta with a little stock, duck meat, the mushroom-basil mixture and Parmesan. Add a little butter every other layer. Cover with foil and bake in the preheated oven for 40–45 minutes, or until cooked. Stand for 10 minutes before serving. Garnish with a sprig of parsley and serve with salad.

Try This: FOR AN ALTERNATIVE: 348   FOR A DIFFERENT MEAT OPTION: 86

Lime & Sesame Turkey

SERVES 4

450 g/1 lb turkey breast, skinned and cut into strips
2 lemon grass stalks (outer leaves discarded), finely sliced
grated zest of 1 lime
4 garlic cloves, peeled and crushed

6 shallots, peeled and finely sliced
2 tbsp Thai fish sauce
2 tsp soft brown sugar
1 small red chilli, deseeded and finely sliced
3 tbsp sunflower oil
1 tbsp sesame oil

225 g/8 oz stir-fry rice noodles
1 tbsp sesame seeds
shredded spring onions, to garnish
freshly stir-fried vegetables, to serve

Place the turkey strips in a shallow dish. Mix together the lemon grass stalks, lime zest, garlic, shallots, Thai fish sauce, sugar and chilli with 2 tablespoons of the sunflower oil and the sesame oil. Pour over the turkey. Cover and leave to marinate in the refrigerator for 2–3 hours, spooning the marinade over the turkey occasionally.

Soak the noodles in warm water for 5 minutes. Drain through a sieve or colander, then plunge immediately into cold water. Drain again and reserve until ready to use.

Heat the wok until very hot and add the sesame seeds. Dry-fry for 1–2 minutes, or until toasted in colour. Remove from the wok and reserve. Wipe the wok to remove any dust left from the seeds.

Heat the wok again and add the remaining sunflower oil. When hot, drain the turkey from the marinade and stir-fry for 3–4 minutes, or until golden brown and cooked through (you may need to do this in 2 batches). When all the turkey has been cooked, add the noodles to the wok and cook, stirring, for 1–2 minutes, or until heated through thoroughly. Garnish with the shredded spring onions and toasted sesame seeds and serve immediately with freshly stir-fried vegetables of your choice.

Try This: FOR AN ALTERNATIVE: 360 FOR A DIFFERENT MEAT OPTION: 186

Turkey Tetrazzini

SERVES 4

275 g/10 oz green and
  white tagliatelle
50 g/2 oz butter
4 slices streaky bacon, diced
1 onion, peeled and
  finely chopped
175 g/6 oz mushrooms,
  thinly sliced

40 g/1½ oz plain flour
450 ml/¾ pint chicken stock
150 ml/¼ pint double cream
2 tbsp sherry
450 g/1 lb cooked turkey meat,
  cut into bite-sized pieces
1 tbsp freshly chopped parsley
freshly grated nutmeg

salt and freshly ground
  black pepper
25 g/1 oz Parmesan
  cheese, grated

To garnish:
freshly chopped parsley
Parmesan cheese, grated

Preheat the oven to 180°C/350°F/Gas Mark 4. Lightly oil a large ovenproof dish. Bring a large saucepan of lightly salted water to the boil. Add the tagliatelle and cook for 7–9 minutes, or until 'al dente'. Drain well and reserve.

In a heavy-based saucepan, heat the butter and add the bacon. Cook for 2–3 minutes, or until crisp and golden. Add the onion and mushrooms and cook for 3–4 minutes, or until the vegetables are tender.

Stir in the flour and cook for 2 minutes. Remove from the heat and slowly stir in the stock. Return to the heat and cook, stirring until a smooth, thick sauce has formed. Add the tagliatelle, then pour in the cream and sherry. Add the turkey and parsley. Season to taste with the nutmeg, salt and pepper. Toss well to coat.

Turn the mixture into the prepared dish, spreading evenly. Sprinkle the top with the Parmesan cheese and bake in the preheated oven for 30–35 minutes, or until crisp, golden and bubbling. Garnish with chopped parsley and Parmesan cheese. Serve straight from the dish.

Try This: FOR AN ALTERNATIVE: 358 FOR A DIFFERENT MEAT OPTION: 74

Creamy Turkey & Tomato Pasta

SERVES 4

4 tbsp olive oil
450 g/1 lb turkey breasts, cut
    into bite-sized pieces
550 g/1¼ lb cherry tomatoes,
    on the vine

2 garlic cloves, peeled
    and chopped
4 tbsp balsamic vinegar
4 tbsp freshly chopped basil
salt and freshly ground

    black pepper
200 ml tub crème fraîche
350 g/12 oz tagliatelle
shaved Parmesan cheese,
    to garnish

Preheat the oven to 200°C/400°F/Gas Mark 6. Heat 2 tablespoons of the olive oil in a large frying pan. Add the turkey and cook for 5 minutes, or until sealed, turning occasionally. Transfer to a roasting tin and add the remaining olive oil, the tomatoes on the vine, garlic and balsamic vinegar. Stir well and season to taste with salt and pepper. Cook in the preheated oven for 30 minutes, or until the turkey is tender, turning the tomatoes and turkey once.

Meanwhile, bring a large pan of lightly salted water to a rolling boil. Add the pasta and cook according to the packet instructions, or until 'al dente'. Drain, return to the pan and keep warm. Stir the basil and seasoning into the crème fraîche.

Remove the roasting tin from the oven and discard the vines. Stir the crème fraîche and basil mix into the turkey and tomato mixture and return to the oven for 1–2 minutes, or until thoroughly heated through.

Stir the turkey and tomato mixture into the pasta and toss lightly together. Tip into a warmed serving dish. Garnish with Parmesan cheese shavings and serve immediately.

Try This: FOR AN ALTERNATIVE: 364 FOR A DIFFERENT MEAT OPTION: 186

Spaghetti with Turkey & Bacon Sauce

SERVES 4

450 g/1 lb spaghetti
25 g /1 oz butter
225 g/8 oz smoked streaky
   bacon, rind removed
350 g/12 oz fresh turkey strips
1 onion, peeled and chopped

1 garlic clove, peeled
   and chopped
3 medium eggs, beaten
300 ml/½ pint double cream
salt and freshly ground
   black pepper

50 g/2 oz freshly grated
   Parmesan cheese
2–3 tbsp freshly chopped
   coriander, to garnish

Bring a large pan of lightly salted water to a rolling boil. Add the spaghetti and cook according to the packet instructions, or until 'al dente'.

Meanwhile, melt the butter in a large frying pan. Using a sharp knife, cut the streaky bacon into small dice. Add the bacon to the pan with the turkey strips and cook for 8 minutes, or until browned, stirring occasionally to prevent sticking. Add the onion and garlic and cook for 5 minutes, or until softened, stirring occasionally.

Place the eggs and cream in a bowl and season to taste with salt and pepper. Beat together then pour into the frying pan and cook, stirring, for 2 minutes or until the mixture begins to thicken but does not scramble.

Drain the spaghetti thoroughly and return to the pan. Pour over the sauce, add the grated Parmesan cheese and toss lightly. Heat through for 2 minutes, or until piping hot. Tip into a warmed serving dish and sprinkle with freshly chopped coriander. Serve immediately.

Try This: FOR AN ALTERNATIVE: 362   FOR A DIFFERENT MEAT OPTION: 276

Baked Aubergines
with Tomato & Mozzarella

SERVES 4

3 medium aubergines,
   trimmed and sliced
salt and freshly ground
   black pepper
4–6 tbsp olive oil
450 g/1 lb fresh turkey mince

1 onion, peeled and chopped
2 garlic cloves, peeled
   and chopped
2 x 400 g cans cherry tomatoes
1 tbsp fresh mixed herbs
200 ml/7 fl oz red wine

350 g/12 oz macaroni
5 tbsp freshly chopped basil
125 g/4 oz mozzarella cheese,
   drained and chopped
50 g/2 oz freshly grated
   Parmesan cheese

Preheat the oven to 200°C/400°F/Gas Mark 6, 15 minutes before cooking. Place the aubergine slices in a colander and sprinkle with salt. Leave for 1 hour or until the juices run clear. Rinse and dry on absorbent kitchen paper.

Heat 3–5 tablespoons of the olive oil in a large frying pan and cook the prepared aubergines in batches for 2 minutes on each side, or until softened. Remove and drain on absorbent kitchen paper.

Heat 1 tablespoon of olive oil in a saucepan, add the turkey mince and cook for 5 minutes, or until browned and sealed. Add the onion to the pan and cook for 5 minutes, or until softened. Add the chopped garlic, the tomatoes and mixed herbs. Pour in the wine and season to taste with salt and pepper. Bring to the boil, lower the heat then simmer for 15 minutes, or until thickened.

Meanwhile, bring a large pan of lightly salted water to a rolling boil. Add the macaroni and cook according to the packet instructions, or until 'al dente'. Drain thoroughly.

Spoon half the tomato mixture into a lightly oiled ovenproof dish. Top with half the aubergine, pasta and chopped basil, then season lightly. Repeat the layers, finishing with a layer of aubergine. Sprinkle with the mozzarella and Parmesan cheeses, then bake in the preheated oven for 30 minutes, or until golden and bubbling. Serve immediately.

 Try This: FOR AN ALTERNATIVE: 360 FOR A DIFFERENT MEAT OPTION: 268

Spatchcocked Poussins with Garlic Sage Butter

SERVES 4

For the herb butter:
6 large garlic cloves
150 g/5 oz butter, softened
2 tbsp freshly snipped chives
2 tbsp freshly chopped sage
juice and grated rind of
   1 small lemon

salt and freshly ground
   black pepper

For the poussins:
4 spatchcocked poussins
2 tbsp extra-virgin olive oil

To garnish:
chives
fresh sage leaves

To serve:
grilled polenta
grilled tomatoes

Preheat the grill or light an outdoor charcoal grill and line the grill rack with foil, just before cooking. Put the garlic cloves in a small saucepan and cover with cold water. Bring to the boil, then simmer for 5 minutes, or until softened. Drain and cool slightly. Cut off the root end of each clove and squeeze the softened garlic into a bowl. Pound the garlic until smooth, then beat in the butter, chives, sage and lemon rind and juice. Season to taste with salt and pepper.

Using your fingertips, gently loosen the skin from each poussin breast by sliding your hand between the skin and the flesh. Push one quarter of the herb butter under the skin, spreading evenly over the breast and the top of the thighs. Pull the neck skin gently to tighten the skin over the breast and tuck under the bird. Repeat with the remaining birds and herb butter.

Thread 2 wooden skewers crossways through each bird, from one wing through the opposite leg, to keep the poussin flat. Repeat with the remaining birds, brush with the olive oil and season with salt and pepper. Arrange the poussins over the foil-lined rack and grill for 25 minutes, turning occasionally, until golden and crisp and the juices run clear when a thigh is pierced with a sharp knife or skewer. (Position the rack about 12.5 cm/5 inches from the heat source or the skin will brown before the birds are cooked through). Garnish with chives and sage leaves and serve immediately with grilled polenta and a few grilled tomatoes.

Try This: FOR AN ALTERNATIVE: 374 FOR A DIFFERENT MEAT OPTION: 154

Guinea Fowl with Calvados & Apples

SERVES 4

4 guinea fowl supremes, each about 150 g/5 oz, skinned
1 tbsp plain flour
1 tbsp sunflower oil
1 onion, peeled and finely sliced
1 garlic clove, peeled and crushed

1 tsp freshly chopped thyme
150 ml/¼ pint dry cider
salt and freshly ground black pepper
3 tbsp Calvados brandy
sprigs of fresh thyme, to garnish

Caramelised apples:
15 g/½ oz unsalted butter
2 red-skinned eating apples, quartered, cored and sliced
1 tsp caster sugar

Lightly dust the guinea fowl supremes with the flour. Heat 2 teaspoons of the oil in a large non-stick frying pan and cook the supremes for 2–3 minutes on each side until browned. Remove from the pan and reserve.

Heat the remaining teaspoon of oil in the pan and add the onion and garlic. Cook over a medium heat for 10 minutes, stirring occasionally until soft and just beginning to colour. Stir in the chopped thyme and cider. Return the guinea fowl to the pan, season with salt and pepper and bring to a very gentle simmer. Cover and cook over a low heat for 15–20 minutes or until the guinea fowl is tender. Remove the guinea fowl and keep warm. Turn up the heat and boil the sauce until thickened and reduced by half.

Meanwhile, prepare the caramelised apples. Melt the butter in a small non-stick pan, add the apple slices in a single layer and sprinkle with the sugar. Cook until the apples are tender and beginning to caramelise, turning once.

Put the Calvados in a metal ladle or small saucepan and heat gently until warm. Carefully set alight with a match, let the flames die down, then stir into the sauce. Serve the guinea fowl with the sauce spooned over and garnished with the caramelised apples and sprigs of fresh thyme.

Try This: FOR AN ALTERNATIVE: 368   FOR A DIFFERENT MEAT OPTION: 184

Pheasant with Portabella Mushrooms & Red Wine Gravy

SERVES 4

25 g/1 oz butter
1 tbsp olive oil
2 small pheasants (preferably hens) rinsed, well dried and halved
8 shallots, peeled
300 g/11 oz portabella mushrooms, thickly sliced

2–3 sprigs of fresh thyme or rosemary, leaves stripped
300 ml/½ pint Valpolicella or fruity red wine
300 ml/½ pint hot chicken stock
1 tbsp cornflour
2 tbsp balsamic vinegar

2 tbsp redcurrant jelly, or to taste
2 tbsp freshly chopped flat-leaf parsley
salt and freshly ground black pepper
sprigs of fresh thyme, to garnish

Preheat the oven to 180°C/350°F/Gas Mark 4. Heat the butter and oil in a large saucepan or frying pan. Add the pheasant halves and shallots, working in batches if necessary, and cook for 10 minutes, or until golden on all sides, shaking the pan to glaze the shallots. Transfer to a casserole dish large enough to hold the pieces in a single layer. Add the mushrooms and thyme to the pan and cook for 2–3 minutes, or until beginning to colour. Transfer to the dish with the pheasant halves.

Add the wine to the saucepan, it will bubble and steam. Cook, stirring up any browned bits from the pan and allow to reduce by half. Pour in the stock and bring to the boil, then pour over the pheasant halves. Cover and braise in the preheated oven for 50 minutes, or until tender. Remove the pheasant halves and vegetables to a wide, shallow serving dish and set the casserole or roasting tin over a medium-high heat.

Skim off any surface fat and bring to the boil. Blend the cornflour with the vinegar and stir into the sauce with the redcurrant jelly. Boil until the sauce is reduced and thickened slightly. Stir in the parsley and season to taste with salt and pepper. Pour over the pheasant halves, garnish with sprigs of fresh thyme and serve immediately.

Try This: FOR AN ALTERNATIVE: 376   FOR A DIFFERENT MEAT OPTION: 280

Pheasant with Sage & Blueberries

SERVES 4

3 tbsp olive oil
3 shallots, peeled and
   coarsely chopped
2 sprigs of fresh sage,
   coarsely chopped
1 bay leaf
1 lemon, halved

salt and freshly ground
   black pepper
2 pheasants or guinea fowl,
   rinsed and dried
125 g/4 oz blueberries
4 slices Parma ham or bacon
125 ml/4 fl oz vermouth or

dry white wine
200 ml/⅓ pint chicken stock
3 tbsp double cream or
   butter (optional)
1 tbsp brandy
roast potatoes, to serve

Preheat oven to 180°C/350°F/Gas Mark 4, 10 minutes before cooking. Place the oil, shallots, sage and bay leaf in a bowl, with the juice from the lemon halves. Season with salt and pepper. Tuck each of the squeezed lemon halves into the birds with 75 g/3 oz of the blueberries, then rub the birds with the marinade and leave for 2–3 hours, basting occasionally.

Remove the birds from the marinade and cover each with 2 slices of Parma ham. Tie the legs of each bird with string and place in a roasting tin. Pour over the marinade and add the vermouth. Roast in the preheated oven for 1 hour, or until tender and golden and the juices run clear when a thigh is pierced with a sharp knife or skewer.

Transfer to a warm serving plate, discard the string and cover with foil. Skim off any surface fat from the tin and set over a medium-high heat. Add the stock to the tin and bring to the boil, scraping any browned bits from the bottom. Boil until slightly reduced. Whisk in the cream or butter, if using, and simmer until thickened, whisking constantly. Stir in the brandy and strain into a gravy jug. Add the remaining blueberries and keep warm.

Using a sharp carving knife, cut each of the birds in half and arrange on the plate with the crispy Parma ham. Serve immediately with roast potatoes and the gravy.

Try This: FOR AN ALTERNATIVE: 372 FOR A DIFFERENT MEAT OPTION: 272

Marinated Pheasant Breasts with Grilled Polenta

SERVES 4

3 tbsp extra-virgin olive oil
1 tbsp freshly chopped
    rosemary or sage leaves
½ tsp ground cinnamon
grated zest of 1 orange
salt and freshly ground

black pepper
8 pheasant or wood
    pigeon breasts
600 ml/1 pint water
125 g/4 oz quick-cook polenta
2 tbsp butter, diced

40 g/1½ oz Parmesan
    cheese, grated
1–2 tbsp freshly
    chopped parsley
assorted salad leaves and
    tomatoes, to serve

Preheat grill just before cooking. Blend 2 tablespoons of the olive oil with the chopped rosemary or sage, cinnamon and orange zest and season to taste with salt and pepper.

Place the pheasant breasts in a large, shallow dish, pour over the oil and marinate until required, turning occasionally.

Bring the water and 1 teaspoon of salt to the boil in a large, heavy-based saucepan. Slowly whisk in the polenta in a thin, steady stream. Reduce the heat and simmer for 5–10 minutes, or until very thick, stirring constantly. Stir the butter and cheese into the polenta, then the parsley and a little black pepper.

Turn the polenta out on to a lightly oiled, non-stick baking tray and spread into an even layer about 2 cm/¾ inch thick. Leave to cool, then chill in the refrigerator for about 1 hour, or until the polenta is chilled. Turn the cold polenta on to a work surface. Cut into 10 cm/4 inch squares. Brush with olive oil and arrange on a grill rack. Grill for 2–3 minutes on each side until crisp and golden, then cut each square into triangles and keep warm.

Transfer the marinated pheasant breasts to the grill rack and grill for 5 minutes, or until crisp and beginning to colour, turning once. Serve the pheasants immediately with the polenta triangles, salad leaves and tomatoes.

Try This: FOR AN ALTERNATIVE: 362   FOR A DIFFERENT MEAT OPTION: 368

Rabbit Italian

SERVES 4

450 g/1 lb diced rabbit, thawed if frozen
6 rashers streaky bacon
1 garlic clove, peeled
1 onion, peeled
1 carrot, peeled

1 celery stalk
25 g/1 oz butter
2 tbsp olive oil
400 g can chopped tomatoes
150 ml/¼ pint red wine
salt and freshly ground

black pepper
125 g/4 oz mushrooms

To serve:
freshly cooked pasta
green salad

Trim the rabbit if necessary. Chop the bacon and reserve. Chop the garlic and onion and slice the carrot thinly, then trim the celery and chop.

Heat the butter and 1 tablespoon of the oil in a large saucepan and brown the rabbit for 5 minutes, stirring frequently, until sealed all over. Transfer the rabbit to a plate and reserve.

Add the garlic, bacon, celery, carrot and onion to the saucepan and cook for a further 5 minutes, stirring occasionally, until softened, then return the rabbit to the saucepan and pour over the tomatoes with their juice and the wine. Season to taste with salt and pepper. Bring to the boil, cover, reduce the heat and simmer for 45 minutes.

Meanwhile, wipe the mushrooms and if large, cut in half. Heat the remaining oil in a small frying pan and sauté the mushrooms for 2 minutes. Drain, then add to the rabbit and cook for 15 minutes, or until the rabbit is tender. Season to taste and serve immediately with freshly cooked pasta and a green salad.

Try This: FOR AN ALTERNATIVE: 380   FOR A DIFFERENT MEAT OPTION: 362

Braised Rabbit with Red Peppers

SERVES 4

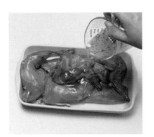

1.1 kg/2½ lb rabbit pieces
125 ml/4 fl oz olive oil
juice and grated zest
    of 1 lemon
2–3 tbsp freshly
    chopped thyme
salt and freshly ground

black pepper
1 onion, peeled and
    thinly sliced
4 red peppers, deseeded
    and cut into 2.5 cm/
    1 inch pieces
2 garlic cloves, peeled

and crushed
400 g can strained,
    crushed tomatoes
1 tsp brown sugar
freshly cooked polenta
    or creamy mashed
    potatoes, to serve

Place the rabbit pieces in a shallow dish with half the olive oil, the lemon zest and juice, thyme and some black pepper. Turn until well coated, then cover and leave to marinate for about 1 hour.

Heat half the remaining oil in a large, heavy-based casserole, add the onion and cook for 5 minutes, then add the peppers and cook for a further 12–15 minutes, or until softened, stirring occasionally. Stir in the garlic, crushed tomatoes and brown sugar and cook, covered, until soft, stirring occasionally.

Heat the remaining oil in a large frying pan, drain the rabbit, reserving the marinade, and pat the rabbit dry with absorbent kitchen paper. Add the rabbit to the pan and cook on all sides until golden. Transfer the rabbit to the casserole and mix to cover with the tomato sauce.

Add the reserved marinade to the frying pan and cook, stirring to loosen any browned bits from the pan. Add to the rabbit and stir gently.

Cover the pan and simmer for 30 minutes or until the rabbit is tender. Serve the rabbit and the vegetable mixture on a bed of polenta or creamy mashed potatoes.

Try This: FOR AN ALTERNATIVE: 378   FOR A DIFFERENT MEAT OPTION: 174

Index

A

Antipasto Penne 258
Apple-tossed Pork 184
Aromatic Duck Burgers on Potato Pancakes 352

B

bacon
   Bacon & Split Pea Soup 230
   Bacon & Tomato Breakfast Twist 228
   Bacon, Mushroom & Cheese Puffs 226
   Lamb's Liver with Bacon & Onions 128
   Sausage & Bacon Risotto 212
   Spaghetti with Turkey & Bacon Sauce 364
Bacon & Split Pea Soup 230
Bacon & Tomato Breakfast Twist 228
Bacon, Mushroom & Cheese Puffs 226
Baked Aubergines with Tomato & Mozzarella 366
Barbecue Pork Steamed Buns 172
Barbecue Pork Fillets 204
Beef & Baby Corn Stir Fry 48
Beef Curry with Lemon & Arborio Rice 56
Beef Fajitas with Avocado Sauce 50
Beef Noodle Soup 28
Beef Teriyaki with Green & Black Rice 70
Beef with Paprika 54
Braised Chicken in Beer 328
Braised Lamb with Broad Beans 156
Braised Rabbit with Red Peppers 380
Brandied Beef 42
Brandied Lamb Chops 120
Brown Rice & Lentil Salad with Duck 354

C

Cannelloni 266
Cannelloni with Spicy Bolognese Filling 90

Cantonese Chicken Wings 294
Caribbean Duck 210
Cashew & Pork Stir Fry 202
Char Sui Pork & Noodle Salad 178
Cheesy Chicken Burgers 336
Chicken & Cashew Nuts 312
Chicken & Lamb Satay 318
Chicken & Red Pepper Curried Rice 316
Chicken Cacciatore 338
Chicken Chow Mein 306
Chicken in Black Bean Sauce 304
Chicken Marengo 342
Chicken Noodle Soup 290
Chicken with Roasted Fennel & Citrus Rice 326
Chicken Wraps 320
Chicken-filled Spring Rolls 292
Chilli Beef 46
Chilli Beef Calzone 58
Chilli Con Carne with Crispy-skinned Potatoes 64
Chilli Lamb 124
Chilli Roast Chicken 334
Chinese Beef with Angel Hair Pasta 106
Chinese-style Fried Rice 250
chop
   Brandied Lamb Chops 120
   Marinated Lamb Chops with Garlic Fried
      Potatoes 148
   Pork Chop Hotpot 264
Chorizo with Pasta in a Tomato Sauce 268
Clear Chicken & Mushroom Soup 286
Coconut Beef 44
Colourful Beef in Lettuce 30
Cornish Pasties 60
Creamed Lamb & Wild Mushroom Pasta 162
Creamy Caribbean Chicken & Coconut Soup 288

Creamy Turkey & Tomato Pasta 362
Crispy Aromatic Duck 346
Crispy Pork with Tangy Sauce 208
Crispy Pork Wontons 168
Crown Roast of Lamb 136

D

Deep-fried Chicken Wings 296
Dim Sum Pork Parcels 180
Duck Lasagne with Porcini & Basil 356
Duck with Berry Sauce 348

F

Fettuccine with Calves' Liver & Calvados 72
Fried Ginger Rice with Soy Glazed Duck 350
Fried Pork-filled Wontons 176
Fried Rice with Chilli Beef 38

G

Gammon with Red Wine Sauce & Pasta 280
Gnocchi & Parma Ham Bake 278
Gnocchi with Tuscan Beef Ragu 108
Grilled Spiced Chicken with Tomato & Shallot
   Chutney 300
Grilled Steaks with Saffron Potatoes & Roast
   Tomato 66
Guinea Fowl with Calvados & Apples 370

H

ham
   Gammon with Red Wine Sauce & Pasta 280
   Gnocchi & Parma Ham Bake 278
   Italian Risotto 260
   Leek & Ham Risotto 240
   Prosciutto & Gruyère Carbonara 282

Hoisin Pork 188
Honey Pork with Rice Noodles & Cashews 216
Hot Salami & Vegetable Gratin 256

I
Italian Beef Pot Roast 98
Italian Calf Liver 100
Italian Meatballs in Tomato Sauce 82
Italian Risotto 260

J
Jamaican Jerk Pork with Rice & Peas 232

K
kidney
    Red Wine Risotto with Lambs' Kidneys &
        Caramelised Shallots 146
Kung-pao Lamb 112

L
Lamb & Meatballs with
    Savoy Cabbage 116
Lamb & Pasta Pie 152
Lamb & Potato Moussaka 134
Lamb Arrabbiata 160
Lamb Pilaf 138
Lamb with Black Cherry Sauce 122
Lamb with Stir-fried Vegetables 114
Lamb's Liver with Bacon & Onions 128
Lancashire Hotpot 142
Leek & Ham Risotto 240
Leg of Lamb with Minted Rice 132
Lemon Chicken 302
Lime & Sesame Turkey 358
Lion's Head Pork Balls 170
liver
    Fettuccine with Calves' Liver & Calvados 72
    Italian Calf Liver 100
    Lamb's Liver with Bacon & Onions 128
    Seared Calves' Liver with

    Onions & Mustard Mash 62
    Tagliatelle with Creamy Liver & Basil 164

M
Marinated Lamb Chops with Garlic Fried Potatoes 148
Marinated Pheasant Breasts with Grilled Polenta 376
meatballs
    Italian Meatballs in Tomato Sauce 82
    Lamb & Meatballs with Savoy Cabbage 116
    Lion's Head Pork Balls 170
    Meatballs with Bean & Tomato Sauce 80
    Meatballs with Olives 76
    Oven-baked Pork Balls with Peppers 262
    Pork Meatballs with Vegetables 190
    Spaghetti & Meatballs 84
    Swedish Cocktail Meatballs 78
Meatballs with Bean & Tomato Sauce 80
Meatballs with Olives 76
Mexican Chicken 340
mince
    Cannelloni 266
    Cannelloni with Spicy Bolognese Filling 90
    Chilli Beef Calzone 58
    Chilli Con Carne with Crispy-skinned
        Potatoes 64
    Gnocchi with Tuscan Beef Ragu 108
    Shepherd's Pie 144
    Spaghetti Bolognese 88
    Spicy Chilli Beef 102
    Traditional Lasagne 86
Moroccan Lamb with Apricots 130
Moroccan Penne 158

N
Nasi Goreng 238
New Orleans Jambalaya 248

O
Orange-roasted Whole Chicken 298
Ossobuco with Saffron Risotto 68

Oven-baked Pork Balls with Peppers 262
Oven-roasted Vegetables with Sausages 254

P
Pan-fried Beef with Creamy Mushrooms 74
Pappardelle Pork with Brandy Sauce 274
Pappardelle with Spicy Lamb & Peppers 150
pasta
    Antipasto Penne 258
    Cannelloni 266
    Cannelloni with Spicy Bolognese Filling 90
    Chinese Beef with Angel Hair Pasta 106
    Chorizo with Pasta in a Tomato Sauce 268
    Creamed Lamb & Wild Mushroom Pasta 162
    Creamy Turkey & Tomato Pasta 362
    Duck Lasagne with Porcini & Basil 356
    Fettuccine with Calves' Liver & Calvados 72
    Gammon with Red Wine Sauce & Pasta 280
    Lamb & Pasta Pie 152
    Moroccan Penne 158
    Pappardelle Pork with Brandy Sauce 274
    Pappardelle with Spicy Lamb & Peppers 150
    Pasta & Pork Ragù 270
    Pasta with Beef, Capers & Olives 104
    Prosciutto & Gruyère Carbonara 282
    Sausage & Redcurrant Pasta Bake 272
    Spaghetti & Meatballs 84
    Spaghetti Bolognese 88
    Spaghetti with Turkey & Bacon Sauce 364
    Tagliatelle with Creamy Liver & Basil 164
    Tagliatelle with Spicy Sausage Ragù 276
    Tagliatelle with Stuffed Pork Escalopes 252
    Traditional Lasagne 86
    Turkey Tetrazzini 360
Pasta & Pork Ragù 270
Pasta with Beef, Capers & Olives 104
Pheasant with Portabella Mushrooms & Red Wine
    Gravy 372
Pheasant with Sage & Blueberries 374
Pork & Cabbage Parcels 206

Pork Chop Hotpot 264
Pork Fried Noodles 186
Pork Goulash & Rice 236
Pork in Peanut Sauce 220
Pork Loin Stuffed with Orange & Hazelnut Rice 234
Pork Meatballs with Vegetables 190
Pork Sausages with Onion Gravy & Best-ever Mash 242
Pork Spring Rolls 198
Pork with Assorted Peppers 224
Pork with Black Bean Sauce 196
Pork with Spring Vegetables & Sweet Chilli Sauce 222
Pork with Tofu 182
Pork with Tofu & Coconut 194
Prosciutto & Gruyère Carbonara 282

R
Rabbit Italian 378
Red Wine Risotto with Lambs' Kidneys & Caramelised Shallots 146
rice
    Beef Curry with Lemon & Arborio Rice 56
    Beef Teriyaki with Green & Black Rice 70
    Brown Rice & Lentil Salad with Duck 354
    Chicken & Red Pepper Curried Rice 316
    Chinese-style Fried Rice 250
    Fried Ginger Rice with Soy Glazed Duck 350
    Fried Rice with Chilli Beef 38
    Italian Risotto 260
    Jamaican Jerk Pork with Rice & Peas 232
    Lamb Pilaf 138
    Leek & Ham Risotto 240
    Leg of Lamb with Minted Rice 132
    Nasi Goreng 238
    New Orleans Jambalaya 248
    Ossobuco with Saffron Risotto 68
    Pork Goulash & Rice 236
    Pork Lion Stuffed with Orange & Hazelnut Rice 234
    Sausage & Bacon Risotto 212

Spanish-style Pork Stew with Saffron Rice 246
Special Fried Rice 200
Sweet-&-Sour Rice with Chicken 322
roast
    Chilli Roast Chicken 334
    Crown Roast of Lamb 136
    Orange Roasted Whole Chicken 298
    Roast Chicken 324
    Roast Cured Pork Loin with Baked Sliced Potatoes 244
    Roast Leg of Lamb & Boulangère Potatoes 140
    Roasted Lamb with Rosemary & Garlic 154
Roast Chicken 324
Roast Cured Pork Loin with Baked Sliced Potatoes 244
Roast Leg of Lamb & Boulangère Potatoes 140
Roasted Lamb with Rosemary & Garlic 154

S
sausage
    Chorizo with Pasta in a Tomato Sauce 268
    Hot Salami & Vegetable Gratin 256
    Italian Risotto 260
    Oven-roasted Vegetables with Sausages 254
    Pork Sausages with Onion Gravy & Best-ever Mash 242
    Sausage & Bacon Risotto 212
    Sausage & Redcurrant Pasta Bake 272
    Tagliatelle with Spicy Sausage Ragù 276
Sausage & Bacon Risotto 212
Sausage & Redcurrant Pasta Bake 272
Sauvignon Chicken & Mushroom Filo Pie 332
Seared Calves' Liver with Onions & Mustard Mash 62
Seared Duck with Pickled Plums 344
Shepherd's Pie 144
Shredded Beef in Hoisin Sauce 34
Shredded Chilli Beef 32
soup
    Bacon & Split Pea Soup 230
    Beef Noodle Soup 28

Chicken Noodle Soup 290
    Clear Chicken & Mushroom Soup 286
    Creamy Caribbean Chicken & Coconut Soup 288
    Vietnamese Beef & Rice Noodle Soup 26
Spaghetti & Meatballs 84
Spaghetti Bolognese 88
Spaghetti with Turkey & Bacon Sauce 364
Spanish-style Pork Stew with Saffron Rice 246
Spatchcocked Poussins with Garlic Sage Butter 368
Special Fried Rice 200
Speedy Pork with Yellow Bean Sauce 214
Spicy Beef Pancakes 24
Spicy Chicken Skewers with Mango Tabbouleh 330
Spicy Chilli Beef 102
Spicy Lamb & Peppers 118
Spicy Lamb in Yoghurt Sauce 126
Spicy Pork 192
Sticky Braised Spareribs 174
Stir-fried Chicken with Basil 310
Stir-fried Beef with Vermouth 52
Stir-fried Chicken with Spinach, Tomatoes & Pine Nuts 314
Swedish Cocktail Meatballs 78
Sweet-&-Sour Pork 218
Sweet-&-Sour Rice with Chicken 322
Sweet-&-Sour Shredded Beef 36
Szechuan Beef 40

T
Tagliatelle with Creamy Liver & Basil 164
Tagliatelle with Spicy Sausage Ragù 276
Tagliatelle with Stuffed Pork Escalopes 252
Thai Coconut Chicken 308
Traditional Lasagne 86
Turkey Tetrazzini 360

V
Veal Escalopes with Marsala Sauce 94
Vietnamese Beef & Rice Noodle Soup 26
Vitello Tonnato (Veal in Tuna Sauce) 96